What people are saying about …

Wait and See

"Most of us have experienced the struggle of wanting something to happen immediately while waiting on God to unfold His plans. If you're in that place now, *Wait and See* will show you you're not alone! Wendy's transparency from her own difficult wait will help take the sting, questioning, and anxiety out of your weary heart. Wendy's book will help keep your faith strong when the wait makes you feel weak."

Lysa TerKeurst, *New York Times* bestselling
author and president of Proverbs 31 Ministries

"Like sweet balm to your soul, Wendy Pope guides you through waiting as if it is the nearest and only way to be in touch with your heavenly Father. If your dream or greatest desire is not yet fulfilled, this is required reading. I absolutely *loved* this book."

Shari Braendel, president of Fashion Meets Faith and
author of *Help Me, Jesus, I Have Nothing to Wear!*

"As a woman who winces when I'm asked to wait, I was encouraged and inspired from the first page of this book to the last! Wendy Pope has skillfully woven together a wealth of Scripture with relevant, real-life stories and powerful passages from the psalms of King David. *Wait and See* goes deep and wide, exposing our need for God and assuring us of His strength. What a comfort to know we never wait alone!"

Liz Curtis Higgs, bestselling author of *Bad Girls of the Bible*

"*Wait and See* is a welcomed equipping tool to help us find security in what can be uncertain times of *waiting*. Wendy builds from biblical truths and applies them to contemporary stories, including her own. By His grace, God has clearly called Wendy to this work by allowing her to live it out. I'm thankful for her faithfulness and willingness to *wait and see* His plan for this book."

Chris Justice, senior pastor of Lee
Park Church, Monroe, NC

"I've grown quite familiar with life's waiting places. Marriage. Parenting six times over. Frightening diagnoses. In every case, the waiting and not knowing turned out to be the most painful part, by far. But what if it doesn't have to be? What if the waiting room became a sacred classroom? With a wealth of personal experience and the wisdom of a lover of God's Word, Wendy Pope will help you turn your waiting place to the place of peace and growth in the safety of God's sure presence."

Michele Cushatt, author of *Undone*

"*Wait and See* is like a chocolate truffle—it must be savored, not devoured, to be fully appreciated. Wendy enables the reader to understand that waiting is not an obstacle to be overcome; rather it is a discipline to be embraced. She weaves sound biblical truths with human experiences to create a pathway for those struggling with the mysteries of waiting, offering practical steps to grasp the fullness of God's purposes in our waits and even in our wilderness times."

John Butler, pastor and chief financial officer of
the Baptist State Convention of North Carolina

From a Focus Group:

"Wendy Pope writes with honesty and vulnerability. Her message in *Wait and See* is one that is sure to resonate with many women. One truth Wendy shares that found its way to my heart was when God appears to be silent, lean closer and press in harder, but never believe He doesn't see or hear your cries. Every woman will be challenged to see her pauses and plans through a different lens. Truly uplifting!"

Lynne Bauman, director of women at Walnut Hill
Community Church and author of *A Heart to Know Him*

"I learned so many valuable lessons about being a woman who waits well from this book. Thank you, Wendy, for teaching me these principles and showing me how to better trust God and have confidence in His timing!"

Elizabeth LaPole

"A diligent steward of Scripture, Wendy accurately and carefully handles the Word of God as she leads us in the journey of faith and trust in the Lord during the waiting seasons of our lives. *Wait and See* encourages us to be quietly and actively patient, to be productive, and to abide in the Lord and deepen our relationship with Him while we wait."

Sharon Sloan, author of *Serendipity*

"Until I read Wendy's *Wait and See*, I really had no idea how to wait well. Wendy examines the waiting process and how to do it well with God at the center of it all. Even though waiting goes against this fast-paced impatient world, Wendy shows us through Scripture and real-life applications the step-by-step action plan for getting ourselves battle ready. *Wait and See* is a life-changing book that will help you see the purpose in your wait. Don't wait to read it!"

Nicole Wells

"Right from the beginning of *Wait and See*, I was captivated by Wendy's transparency and humility. Her vulnerability and insight into God's Word allowed me to examine areas in my life where I have replaced worshipping God with the object of my wait. Wendy's love for God and His Word becomes contagious as you read through *Wait and See*, and it made me want to dive deeper into the Bible. I have no doubt that *Wait and See* will definitely become one of those books you read and reread throughout your Christian walk, and it will be the one you will to recommend to others."

Linda Schoch

"In a culture of instant access and instant gratification, we have lost the ability to appreciate *the wait*. How often do we miss out on the present because we are so focused on the future? Wendy has found the key to learning how to wait well, to trust God's timing, and to find peace in the unknown. *Wait and See* came at the perfect time in my life and blessed me with the ability to learn and grow closer to the Lord instead of missing out on the blessing of my own wait."

Shelley Summerville

Wait and See

Wait and See

Finding Peace in God's Pauses and Plans

Wendy Pope

David C. Cook

transforming lives together

WAIT AND SEE
Published by David C Cook
4050 Lee Vance Drive
Colorado Springs, CO 80918 U.S.A.

David C Cook U.K., Kingsway Communications
Eastbourne, East Sussex BN23 6NT, England

The graphic circle C logo is a registered trademark of David C Cook.

The website addresses recommended throughout this book are offered as a
resource to you. These websites are not intended in any way to be or imply an
endorsement on the part of David C Cook, nor do we vouch for their content.

Details in some stories have been changed to protect
the identities of the persons involved.

Bible credits are listed at the back of this book.
The author has added italics to Scripture quotations for emphasis.

LCCN 2016946269
ISBN 978-0-7814-1355-8
eISBN 978-1-4347-1096-3

© 2016 Wendy Pope

The Team: Tim Peterson, Keith Wall, Nick Lee, Jack Campbell, Susan Murdock
Cover Design: Amy Konyndyk
Cover Photo: iStock

Printed in the United States of America
First Edition 2016

4 5 6 7 8 9 10 11 12

110216

To my amazing family:
Scott, Blaire, and Griffin.
Thank you for waiting with me.

Contents

Foreword

It was October 2009, and after two long years of wading through endless paperwork, saying countless prayers, crying many tears, and wondering if our adoption would ever happen, we finally brought home our ten-month-old baby girl from Ethiopia.

Our long wait was over! And our new life together as a family of five was finally here.

A few weeks later, my mom called early one morning to tell us she couldn't breathe and needed someone to take her to the hospital. My husband rushed her to the emergency room, while I scrambled to get our kids taken care of. Later that morning, my mom was hospitalized with pulmonary embolisms.

In addition to blood clots in both lungs, Mom developed a kidney infection caused by a kidney stone so large it required surgery to remove it. When my mom was released from the hospital eight days later, she moved in with our family instead of going home.

A month later, my annual mammogram came back abnormal. I was immediately scheduled for two biopsies the week after Christmas and referred to an oncologist for genetic testing because of my family's extensive history of breast cancer.

The same afternoon of my appointment, my brother called from Florida to say our dad had been to the doctor that day because of chest pains. Tests revealed severe blockage, and Dad was scheduled for emergency quadruple bypass heart surgery that week.

I had thought our long wait was over, when in reality I was walking into another season of waiting …

Waiting to see what the future held for my mom.

Waiting to see if my dad would make it through open-heart surgery.

Waiting to see if my biopsies would indicate I had cancer.

While I waited on God to show me what to do, I wrote these words in my journal:

> Lord, my heart is in a wobbly place, teetering between fear and faith. Jesus, please infuse my soul with courage to trust Your ways and Your timing.
>
> Lord, I don't want cancer. I don't want to settle for believing it is my destiny just because it is in my history. The past doesn't define my future—You do. You are the One who knows the plans You have for me, plans to prosper me and not to harm me, plans to give me a future and a hope. Oh, Jesus, this is my hope: that You are good, that You are loving, that You are able and willing to heal and restore, to redeem and remake.
>
> I stand at the foot of the cross knowing I must lay down my body before You. I want to be willing

to let You work in my life through whatever circumstances You allow. Like so many other times before, it is in my suffering I see and share in Your glory. And isn't that what I was made for? I want to be a reflection of Your glory, a representation of who You are. Father, make me a willing vessel to surrender and rest in You, no matter what. I pray You will keep my heart in perfect peace, because my mind is steadfast as I trust in You. No matter what tomorrow brings, may You find me faithfully available to lay it all down before You as a sacrificial offering of praise.

I wish I could tell you I prayed those words and lived them faithfully from that day forward. But I didn't. Yet when my trust wavered, I recognized my only hope was to return to this place of surrender, again and again. And when my biopsy results came back negative, I thanked God for that answer to prayer and the ways He was molding my heart through it all.

Waiting is inevitable. Waiting with hope and courage is optional.

If we want to wait well and experience all God has for us in the midst of our waiting, we have to be honest with Him about our fears and struggles. We also have to ask Jesus to give us eyes to see through a lens of hope and a heart molded by faith that He is working for our good and His glory.

Through the pages of *Wait and See*, my friend Wendy Pope will help you do just that. Chapter by chapter, she will help you look for God and find Him in the middle of your wait.

What I love about Wendy is that she doesn't just tell us to "be patient and trust God." She shows us how. With the wisdom and compassion of a trusted friend, Wendy walks with us each step of the way, guiding our hearts into a place of strength and perseverance as we learn to see God's handiwork, the evidence of His presence, and the gift of His peace that "waiting well" brings.

Renee Swope
Word-lover | Story-teller | Grace-needer
Author of *A Confident Heart*

Acknowledgments

To Renee: I don't know if this book would have been written had you not followed the Spirit's leading. You courageously spoke the words that changed the course of my writing pursuits. I am blessed by your foreword and honored to have you as part of my first published project. Love you, friend!

To the Wait and See Group: Cindy, Elizabeth, Jane, Karen, Linda, Lynne, Nicole, Sharon, Shelley, Susan, and Tracy. Y'all are simply the best! Your feedback, all of it, positive and polishing, was invaluable in the shaping of the book. I can never repay you for the time you sacrificed, so I pray God's greatest blessings on you and your families. Is this a good time to ask for your help with the next book?

To the Waiters: thank you, Ashley, Samantha, Diana, and Scott for sharing your wait and your struggles. Your transparency will bless and encourage everyone who reads *Wait and See*. Glynnis, C. T. and Becky, Heather, and Chad, your stories put the perfect finishing touch to chapter 9.

To my team at David C Cook: I love my publishing home in Colorado! Cris, Verne, and Kyle, you took a chance on a first-time author. Thank you for believing in the message. Tim Peterson, I remember leaving our first meeting at She Speaks hopeful of things to come. Thank you for all you did to bring my publishing wait to a beautiful end. Your kind heart was amplified in your edits. I can't wait (no pun intended) until our next project. Chriscynethia, Tim Close, Annette, Darren, and Lisa, you have done an amazing job of getting the word out about *Wait and See*. Now we get to *wait* and *see* how God will bless your talents and efforts. Amy and Jon, the cover is refreshing and inviting, bringing the title to life. Thank you for allowing me to be part of the process.

To Blythe Daniel: you are undoubtedly the greatest agent an author could ever dream of working with. You care about every aspect of your clients' success. You have talked me off the ledge more than once. I remember the day I called to say, "I'm done. I think I am supposed to read the Bible and teach RTW. I've had enough rejections. Just tell me we have exhausted all our options so I can lay this down." You wouldn't hear of it. You tenderly encouraged me to hang in there and *wait* for the right project and God's timing. Professionally, you have exceeded my expectations. Personally, you have blessed me beyond words. Thank you for never giving up on me and not allowing me to give up on me.

To Samantha: as the supereditor, your fingerprints are on every page of *Wait and See*. From our first breakfast meeting at Chick-fil-A, you believed in the message and caught the vision. Your support and encouragement both personally and professionally have meant more to me than you will ever know. You beautifully steward the gifts God has given you. You have made me a better writer. It's an honor to call you editor and friend. I can't wait to get started on the next project!

To Meggy and Nicki: our writing retreats are full of memories that I will treasure forever. We have shared miles, meals, laughter, tears, and words—lots of words. You loved and supported me when I didn't think I could go on. Nicki, I celebrate this year with you us as we release our first books. We did it! Meg, I can't wait to throw confetti at your book launch party. You have a message that needs to be heard. God's timing is perfect. Don't stop writing! I love you both dearly!

To Christie: you know my deepest secrets and love me anyway. I can't imagine, nor do I want to imagine, what my life might have been like had you chosen Beverly instead of me under the magnolia tree that day in preschool. You've kept me grounded through some dark days. I love our morning drive-time chats. Thank goodness for unlimited text and talk. Being your bestie is one of the greatest joys in my life. Thank you for waiting with me! I love you!

To my parents: Daddy, you are the greatest man I know. Without words, you taught me the importance of God's Word. At night, through the slats on the folding door, when you didn't know I was looking, I saw you reading your Bible. And every time I climbed into the cab of the truck, I noticed your small red New Testament on the dashboard. Thank you for showing me the way and for praying for me every day. I am who I am because of the example you and Momma set for me. Y'all set the bar high. I pray I can reach it.

Momma, I know I am the writer, but words fail me right now. I'll let God's Word speak for me. This is Proverbs 31:25–31 from The Living Bible (the green one I always saw in front of you at the breakfast table):

She is a woman of strength and dignity and has no fear of old age. When she speaks, her words are wise, and kindness is the rule for everything she says. She watches carefully all that goes on throughout her household and is never lazy. Her children stand and bless her; so does her husband. He praises her with these words: "There are many fine women in the world, but you are the best of them all!"

Charm can be deceptive and beauty doesn't last, but a woman who fears and reverences God shall be greatly praised. Praise her for the many fine things she does. These good deeds of hers shall bring her honor and recognition from people of importance.

Today I stand and bless you!

To Scott, Blaire, and my G-Man: being a wife and momma are my highest callings. My life is complete with the three of you by my side. You have each, in your own individual way, supported me through this wait. Griffin: thank you for making me laugh, such as when you replaced the crème in the Oreo with toothpaste. You are my comic relief! Blaire: thank you for your editorial skills and encouragement. You read and reread chapters with a critical eye. I thank you for pushing me to excellence. You are brave to allow me to share your story. I know that God will bless you and encourage many through your words. Scott: you've always believed in me, even when I didn't believe in myself. Thank you for teaching me to dream and helping me reach high.

Introduction

Learning to Wait and See

A teacher. A wife. A mother. My little-girl heart dreamed of being all of these one day.

With chalk in hand and glasses resting on my nose, I practiced being a teacher with my stuffed animals. Carol Brady of *The Brady Bunch* taught me all I needed to know about being a wife. Caring for my dolls, as well as my years of babysitting, prepared me for motherhood. When I graduated from high school, I was ready to put my plans in motion.

Becoming a teacher requires four years of college. Graduated. Got a job. Dream came true.

Becoming a wife requires a fella. Found and dated him for two years. Got a husband. Dream came true.

Becoming a mother requires ... well, you know what it requires. No details are necessary. After two years of trying, no baby. Dream didn't come true.

My first two dreams came to pass just as *I* had planned. However, after the two years of failing to conceive, I wondered if I would ever sing the childhood rhyme, "First comes love, then comes marriage, then comes Wendy with a baby carriage." Dream number three required me to wait and see.

You need to know something about me: I have never been a wait-and-see kind of girl. Deep down, I am a hurry-up, right-now, please-and-thank-you kind of gal. The word *patient* does not describe me—ask anyone who knows and loves me. So you can imagine how well I handled waiting to see my dream of motherhood come true. Waiting dominated my thoughts as it does for most of us when we're waiting for the fulfillment of our hopes and dreams.

And you? Do you feel the tug of waiting for something but are scared to let yourself dream it will happen? Maybe you are waiting on a miracle. We have all been there—sometimes more often than we prefer. And the miracle requires something of us—waiting.

TIMING REALLY IS EVERYTHING

The desire to be a mother consumed me and my thoughts. *Why can't I get pregnant? What is wrong with me? What have I done to warrant such punishment from God?* It seemed my girlfriends were getting pregnant with ease. That just didn't seem fair, so I determined that God wasn't fair.

I began to decline invitations to the multitude of blue-and-pink parties. My husband and I purposely socialized with friends who were not expecting or didn't have children. However, avoiding pregnant friends did not ease my pain or subdue my longing.

What have I done to warrant such punishment from God?

Trying harder didn't help either. For two years, I ingested fertility pills, endured monthly injections, scheduled intimacy, and charted my basal body thermometer readings every morning at six o'clock. There wasn't a specialist or a test that could explain why I was unable to conceive.

Medically, I was doing everything right; spiritually, I was not. The wait exhausted my faith.

I resolved that God was mad at me, so I resolved to be mad at Him in return. Maybe you can relate? You still go to church on Sunday but have nothing to do with God on the other days ending in *y*. We have *our* plans and want *our* way. When things don't happen accordingly, we retaliate by ignoring God. I felt this way for over two years as the object of my wait became greater than the Person of my faith.

THE WAIT AND SEE

Eventually, I did conceive.

Had my faith matured and had I patiently waited for God's plan to unfold? Had I accepted a potentially childless future with grace? That would be a great big resounding *no*! I'd love to say I learned to trust God more, regularly devoured what I was learning in Bible study, and served others during the wait. Unfortunately, none of these are even close to the truth. When I became pregnant with my daughter, I was far from God and indifferent toward Him. His attempts to communicate with me through whispers from Scripture and the sensing of His Spirit during worship songs at church were ignored. It is safe to say I wasn't on speaking terms with the Lord.

It's now been almost twenty years since that difficult season, and I've learned this key point: Waiting well looks forward to the *future* while staying present in the *present*. Waiting well means I remain open to God and allow Him to move me toward the future He has planned, in His time. I did not wait well.

You see, staying present in the present required me to be happy for others who were living my dream, even as I felt every ache of not having a child. Staying present meant accepting that questions would remain unanswered. Staying present should have involved my being content with the here and now and whatever the future held. But I could not bear to look forward to the future, because as far as I could see, my future was childless. And a childless future was not a future I wanted.

> **Waiting well looks forward to the future**
> **while staying present in the present.**

It took me a few years, but eventually I learned that the conception of my daughter had occurred in God's perfect timing. All of our "wait and see" experiences do. I envision Him running His finger across the kingdom calendar in December 1996, saying, "Yep. It's time." If we are willing to learn, the wait and see can be full of valuable lessons.

Maybe you are currently in a wait-and-see season that seems as though it will never end: waiting on a job, the return of a wayward child, your husband's salvation, a man to marry, or a job promotion. Or perhaps you have just come out of one waiting season and believe you are headed into another. Waiting is hard. In the wait and see, it is imperative that we pause to consider the possibilities of God's design. From the depths of our ache, can we dare say to Him, "Show me what You have planned. I am willing to wait"?

When we ask God to show us His plan, we begin to align our heart with His heart. The door opens to experience God in deeper, more real ways. We still wait, but we deepen our knowledge of His character and goodness. We learn to trust that God acts on behalf of those who are willing to wait and see (Isa. 64:4) and that He does immeasurably more than we can think or imagine (Eph. 3:20). As we wait, we find peace in God's plans and hope in His pauses. Our focus moves from the object of our wait to the Person of our faith.

READY TO WAIT AND SEE

God has graciously brought you and me together to look at His faithfulness through the experiences of everyday women and the life of King David. We'll glean truth from David's life that will help us become women who wait well and see God's goodness in the pauses.

Can I encourage you before we get started? All of my dreams haven't come true, and plenty of my plans haven't come to fulfillment. In fact, I've been in a wait and see for over twenty years for something so dear to my heart that only God knows. Is every day a breeze? Honestly, no. But I can say after decades of waiting I've learned that some of our sweetest encounters with God are during our wait-and-see seasons.

You might be asking, "How can waiting bring about sweet encounters with God? It doesn't feel sweet when Sunday after

Sunday I load the children into the car for church and try to explain to them why Daddy doesn't go. 'Sweet' is not how I would describe the walk back to the treatment room. I don't feel closer to God as I stare at my empty checking account, waiting for the deposit of another unemployment check. How can waiting bring me close to God?"

These seasons are not passive times of inactivity, waiting around until our circumstances change. The wait and see is a time of action, excitement, and joy when we join God in His plans for our life (yes, even on the days we don't want to get out of bed and face our circumstances).

Let's join our God in the wait-and-see adventure. The adventure may take us to the place we have set our hopes on or a place we never expected, but we can have complete confidence to trust Him for an outcome that will bring us good and glorify Him.

As I studied Scripture in preparation for writing this book, my heart softened toward the Lord. I came to see His pauses as a safeguard and comfort. I came to view Him as a trustworthy advocate. He is for me. He is for you.

My prayer is that your heart will go through a similar transformation. The anxiety over your future will change to living peacefully in God's pauses as you wait for Him to fulfill His plans. Instead of living in the shadow of depression, doubt, and discouragement, you will bask in the light of hope, trust, and security. And rather than striving on your own, you will learn how to participate in God's work in the present. As we reach the end of our journey, you'll be prepared to confidently trust in God's plans for your future.

DIGGING DEEPER WITH DAVID

Every chapter in this book features a short, in-depth study of a psalm written by David. Each study will give us greater insight to David's wait. We will feel his heartbeat as he anxiously hides in the cave of Adullam. We will sense the rejection he feels when Saul turns on him. And, oh, how we will celebrate as he is finally crowned king of Israel.

Sometimes when I'm reading a book, I tend to skip over the study portion, determining to come back to it later. Do you ever do that? If so, I'd encourage you to pause before moving on to the next chapter. Take time to reflect on this section and answer the questions. You will find the scriptures uplifting and inspiring. Our ultimate goal is to focus on the Person of our faith more than the object of our wait. The "Digging Deeper with David" studies will guide us in doing just that.

I can't wait to study God's Word with you!

A SPECIAL FEATURE

As much as I love Bible study, perhaps my favorite feature of *Wait and See* is the active role you will have as we travel through the pages. *Wait and See* is a real-time reader-participatory book. You are more than a reader; you are a participant in a journey. You will do more than read chapters and answer Bible study questions.

Wait and See gives you the opportunity for real-life change as you apply God's truth to your real-life circumstances. You get to write the final chapter! Isn't that fun? Wait. Did panic just fill your body? Are you already thinking of excuses like, "I'm not an author. I've never written anything. I'm a terrible speller." Your only audience is you and God (and maybe a friend if you decide to share what God teaches you).

At the conclusion of each chapter is a section called This Principle in Your Pause. In it, I provide writing prompts that summarize the principles outlined in the chapter. After reading the prompt, you will turn to chapter 10, "Worth the Wait: My Story," and respond.

Your participation starts now. "Worth the Wait" is full of blank lines waiting (no pun intended) to be filled with your story. There is plenty of room for misspelled words, incorrect grammar, and imperfection. It's okay if the pages become tear stained as you pour out your heart to the God who loves you. He is ready to hear from you regarding your deepest desire, that one thing you have been waiting for.

You may adore the idea of writing in your book … or you may dislike it! If journaling on the pages of this book doesn't appeal to you, that's no problem. Feel free to write your thoughts and answers in a notebook or type them on your computer or phone—whatever works for you.

Are you ready to join God in the pages of *Wait and See*?

THIS PRINCIPLE IN YOUR PAUSE

Turn to chapter 10, "Worth the Wait," and write about a current wait that you are experiencing.

1

When the Wait Begins

Meet Ashley, Samantha, Dianna, Scott (my husband), and David. These are real people who waited on God. As we journey together, you will see how each individual applied the principles of waiting well.

When she was thirty years old, Ashley sensed God leading her to teach women the Bible. Thinking she had it all figured out and certain of God's desire for her life, Ashley jumped right in to preparing her Bible study class at church. She organized her materials, started the sign-up process, and counted on God to fill her classroom. Only one woman joined, and she later withdrew because of a scheduling conflict. Did Ashley hear God wrong?

God shows you His design for your life. He whets your appetite for all He has planned. Excitement overwhelms you as you sit on the edge of your seat. Then you wait.

Ashley waited.

In her early twenties, Samantha began to seriously ponder if it was the Lord's will for her to be married. She felt Him give her a green light, so she prayed daily for her marriage and her husband—even though she didn't yet know him. She studied scriptures on marriage and about being a wife, and she gleaned wisdom from many married women. Year after year, Samantha continued hoping for a husband, trusting that her desires to marry were from the Lord. Yet year after year, she remained single.

God tucks a dream deep into your heart. You believe Him for the completion of this dream. You patiently do all the "right" things. Then you wait.

Samantha waited.

Dianna felt the call to full-time ministry. With her husband's job secure, she walked away from a $75,000-a-year career to pursue her calling. Her *yes* to God was followed by the 2008 market crash, which devastated her family. Her husband, a builder of custom homes, lost his job. Losing their own home was just the start of some tough years of waiting and rebuilding. During the family's five moves, including a two-month stay in a hotel, Dianna contracted severe acute respiratory syndrome (SARS). Things looked hopeful when the family found a wonderful home to rent—only to receive an eviction notice because the landlord had not paid the mortgage. Facing homelessness again, a disease, no health insurance, and no job, Dianna felt betrayed, helpless, abandoned, and hopeless.

The timing seems right. You step out in faith and say yes to God, then you lose your home and health.

Dianna waited.

Scott stood six foot three—a strong, healthy man. He and I were busy doing life and raising our two children. Everything seemed picture perfect for our family. Without warning, the picture became blurred, literally, when the vision in Scott's left eye began to fail. He went from one specialist to another. Each doctor ordered new tests and, with the best intentions, prescribed new treatments. We prayed for healing. Our church family rallied around us and prayed. I invited my blog friends to pray. We had people all over the world asking God to heal Scott's eye. Yet after eighteen months, there was still no definitive diagnosis or change in Scott's condition.

You pray. You anoint with oil. You pray some more. Then you wait. We waited.

Jesse was a farmer and breeder in Bethlehem. David was the youngest of his eight sons, who worked the land with their father. Can you imagine if any hopes or dreams were left for you when you're the youngest of eight?

The prophet Samuel called on Jesse to anoint one of his sons as the next king of Israel. Jesse brought each son one by one to Samuel. After meeting the boys, Samuel still had not heard God's voice of confirmation. The prophet asked Jesse if he had any more sons. Imagine Jesse's internal response: *Um, this isn't my hope or plans for David. He's just a shepherd boy. He deserves to stay home.* Jesse answered truthfully and called David from the pasture.

> Then the LORD said, "Rise and anoint him; this is the one."
>
> So Samuel took the horn of oil and anointed him in the presence of his brothers, and from that day on the Spirit of the LORD came powerfully upon David. Samuel then went to Ramah. (1 Sam. 16:12–13)

I can only imagine what might have been going on inside of David's mind (and Jesse's). David did not dream of being king. He thought his life's path had already been chosen for him: he would be a farmer and breeder, just like his father and brothers. But God's plan for David's life was different. Samuel appointed and anointed David king of Israel, but David wouldn't fulfill that position for many years.

David waited.

Do you see yourself somewhere between the lines of these waiting stories? Maybe you are praying for a husband or waiting for God's plan for your life to come to fruition. Perhaps your life has fallen into place just as God revealed but something or someone is blocking the way toward what you really hope for. So you wait, hope, believe, and yet sometimes second-guess the plan.

> ***The wait is more about experiencing***
> ***God than enduring the delay.***

WANTING AND WAITING

I don't know anyone who likes to wait. Life in our technologically advanced world has taught us that waiting does not have to be an option. Let's face it—within seconds of posting to Instagram and Facebook, everyone can see pictures of your lunch with your best friend.

Snapchat allows us to instantly picture chat with anyone, anywhere, anytime. Text messaging is faster than a telephone call, and email is quicker than the postal service. Our dinner can be paid for, cooked, and placed in our hands in a matter of minutes without us even leaving our car. Yes, the message we've received from our have-it-your-way world is "You don't have to wait." But, friend, we have been deceived.

We may want our food served quickly; however, in waiting we are more likely to be served healthier food that's better for us. I am sure at one time or another we all have burned with an urgency to express our thoughts in an email, text message, or Facebook update concerning something that has made us angry. On the other hand, if we push through the want with a timely wait, we have the opportunity to thoughtfully respond so others will see Christ in us. Can we collectively agree things usually turn out better when we wait?

When I was young, my family had one television. My brother and I had to take turns watching our favorite television shows. This got old fast, so I decided it would be nice for me to have my very own television in my bedroom. I took this bright idea to my parents. To my surprise, they said yes, but they wisely turned my want into a wait.

Instead of buying the television for me, they made me earn the money. After months of babysitting and doing extra chores, I finally saved the eighty-nine dollars needed to purchase the thirteen-inch, black-and-white set. While sitting on *my* bed, watching *my* favorite shows, without my older brother pestering me, I determined that small television I had wanted so much to be worth the wait.

As adults, the value of what we wait for is far greater than the cost of a black-and-white television. We wait for the salvation of our loved one, the healing of our friend, the end of our own long-term health issue, deliverance from addiction, a positive result on a pregnancy test, or the end of unemployment. The value of what we wait for is so great that we can easily become derailed from life.

These things are important to pray about, for sure. But when they become all consuming, their value is magnified—especially the longer we wait. Some carry greater weight than we originally thought, while some carry less. As the days, months, and years pass, we can put more energy, effort, prayer, conversations, and, yes, sometimes manipulation and guilt trips into making these things come to pass. We easily become derailed, sacrificing our time with the Lord, relationships with loved ones, and enjoyment of life in general. When we do, we become bankrupt: spiritually, mentally, emotionally, and sometimes even financially. When we value the things we wait on more than we value the commands of the Lord—not to worry, to accept His peace, to live by faith—we lose sight of what's really important: our relationship with God. Without realizing it, we exchange the Person of our faith for the object of our wait.

THE PERSON OF OUR FAITH

Too often, we consult the Person of our faith (God) only after we have exhausted our efforts to push through our wait on our own. If we want to be women who wait well, we will invite God to be part of the process at the beginning, setting our focus on the Lord, not that for which we are waiting. In Scripture, we see the prophet Isaiah helped the Israelites turn their focus on God with a promise. A woman waiting can adjust the lens of her focus with the same truth.

> Since ancient times no one has heard,
> no ear has perceived,

> no eye has seen any God besides you,
>
> who acts on behalf of those who wait for Him.
>
> (Isa. 64:4)

This invitation is an act of surrender and does not deemphasize the worth of her husband's salvation, a friend's healing, or anything else she's waiting on. The invitation directs the lens of her hopes, desires, and dreams to her great God, rather than the object of her wait.

What encouraging words! God is speaking to His people concerning their restoration after seventy years of captivity in Babylon. Although this verse is about Israel's return to Jerusalem, we can find ourselves in the reference to "those who wait." We share in the hope that no ear has perceived, no eye has seen. That means we are the benefactors of something that no one has ever seen or heard when we wait on God. Now that is shoutin' worthy news right there (insert your own shouts and amens here)!

The news gets better as we find the word *prepared* used in the King James Version of Isaiah 64:4, "For since the beginning of the world men have not heard, nor perceived by the ear, neither hath the eye seen, O God, beside thee, what he hath *prepared* for him that waiteth for him." "Prepared" is the Hebrew word *asah*, which means "to do" or "make" in the broadest sense and widest application. "Those who wait" have access to unlimited and mind-blowing futures when they are willing to wait on God to work on their behalf. That bears repeating: in the broadest sense and widest application. If you weren't shoutin' before, you should be now! This truth is the first of many we'll discover that will change our perspective about waiting.

We all know the unlimited, mind-blowing lengths
that God went to in creating our world.

As my son would say, "There's always a catch." The unlimited and mind-blowing future God has for us has a prerequisite: we are required to wait.

"Wait" in Isaiah 64:4 is the Hebrew word *khaw-kaw'*. God teaches us through the word *khaw-kaw'* to tarry for Him to act on our behalf. This means "those who wait" are to delay in acting or starting anything. Waiters are to linger where they are, doing what they know to do until they receive instructions.

Words such as *delay* and *linger* don't sit well in the spirit of a girl like me who prefers to move, take action, and make things happen. However, as we delay and linger, we can know for certain the future we move toward is from the hand of God, not by means of manipulation or anything we can add to the equation. What a relief! We don't have to do anything to get what only God wants to bring us. Isn't that awesome to remember?

The Hebrew word *khaw-kaw'* helps us understand that waiting for God is not laziness. Waiting for God is not going to sleep. Waiting for God is not the abandonment of effort. Waiting for God means, first, activity under His command. Second, it means readiness for any new command that may come: we pray for His direction. Third, waiting involves the ability to do nothing until the command is given.[1] Honestly, all of this sounds well and good on paper, but we all know waiting isn't easy and waiting well is even more difficult. As our wait begins, our mind conjures up all manner of fallacies and misunderstandings. But equipping ourselves with these truths will empower us to do what seems impossible—to wait well.

WAITING MISCONCEPTIONS

When times get hard and the wait seems too long, we begin to doubt God as well as the unlimited and mind-blowing future He has planned for us. We begin to question God: *Did I hear You correctly? Do You see what I am going through? Why does this have to be so hard?* We blame God because our circumstances seem more difficult than before we invited Him into our wait. It is during these times that we have to fight to maintain our focus on the Person of our faith rather than the object of wait or distracting circumstances that surround us. One way to do this is through prayer.

The Lord longs for us to reach out to Him and ask for help, clarity, and direction. See what James 1:5–8 says: "If you don't know what you're doing, pray to the Father. He loves to help. You'll get his help, and won't be condescended to when you ask for it. Ask boldly, believingly, without a second thought. People who 'worry their prayers' are like wind-whipped waves. Don't think you're going to get anything from the Master that way, adrift at sea, keeping all your options open" (THE MESSAGE). In this verse, James clearly tells us we are to ask our Father for what we need. James says God *loves* to help. I certainly like the sound of that—how about you?

Let's keep this verse handy as we revisit and expand on the wait-and-see stories (of Ashley, Samantha, Dianna, Scott, and David) from earlier in the chapter to identify common misconceptions "those who wait" encounter. Recognizing these misconceptions will empower us to wait well, stay present in the present, and experience God in our delay. Notice how each person asked for and experienced God's help along the way.

Ashley sensed God moving her toward teaching a Bible study. She prepared and did everything necessary to give the class a great start. But all her efforts seemingly went unnoticed and were in vain. When it was time for the class to start, she didn't have any students to teach.

Misconception #1: If I am waiting, I must not have heard God correctly. Ashley learned that waiting doesn't necessarily mean you heard God incorrectly. Ashley says, "We give up too easily because we don't see what we want to see when we want to see it."

We can redirect the negative thoughts we often receive by revisiting the moments when we sensed the Lord's nudging. Reliving the moments of pure excitement we experienced when we felt the prodding of His Spirit will extinguish uncertainty that tries to creep in to steal our joy. We may have to travel down memory lane many times during our wait. Ashley had to make the trip several times throughout her ten-year pause, asking for God's clarity and assurance.

This is why it is so important to invite God into our wait from the very beginning, instead of after we have tried everything we know to make things happen. As we spend time with Him and in His Word, we gain confidence in His plans. A quick visit to the past fills us with the peace we need to make it through the pause. Waiting well teaches us to trust His delays rather than doubt His ways.

Misconception #2: If I am waiting, I must desire something not in God's will for my life. Samantha desired to be married. She knew God ordained and approved marriage, but did He want *her* to be married? There are plenty of verses in the Bible about marriage, relationships, and how to be a loving spouse. Yet Samantha also knew the verses in which Paul clearly states that some people are called to remain single. When passages seemingly conflict, it can be difficult to determine God's will for your life.

Samantha asked her family and several close friends to pray for her. She committed to taking each step she felt God asked of her—whether that was toward meeting her future spouse or remaining single.

> *We need to prepare in the pauses so we're*
> *ready to embrace God's plans.*

Misconception #3: If I am waiting, I must not be praying enough. Day after day, Dianna prayed and sought the Lord. Many days, she ate only one meal so her family could have all the food they needed. She watched her husband take odd jobs here and there just to make ends meet. Dianna spent weekends at the laundromat because she did not have a washer or a dryer. She fought the spirit of discouragement on her knees.

She knew in her heart God would supply their needs, but she had to keep telling her head. Dianna faithfully followed the teaching of Paul in 1 Thessalonians 5:17: "Never stop praying" (NLT). Her wait didn't end because she prayed, but her resolve strengthened, helping her to face each day.

Misconception #4: If I am waiting, I must not have enough faith. This was the lie I believed as we agonized over Scott's declining health. His faith is quiet and personal. As we lived out this mystery, I watched his discreet faith become deathly silent. His attitude toward prayer and the things of God grew cynical.

While Scott's faith is quiet, mine is vocal. When I wasn't serving or teaching at church, I was leading women's conferences and writing devotions and book contributions. My prayer life and Bible study were more than routine. Each morning, I had, and still have, a standing appointment with the Lord. Certainly I was doing enough work for the kingdom to get God's attention concerning Scott's health. All of this surely proved my faith was strong enough for the two of us and was worthy of a little healing.

What was I doing wrong? Was God holding my past against me? Had I not done enough to earn His favor? Sometimes waiting has less to do with the strength of your faith and more to do with the perfection of God's timing.

Here's the thing—I *should* have prayed and read my Bible, but not to work my way back into God's good graces. He is a gracious and merciful God. My praying and Scripture reading do not make Him more gracious. Somewhere along the way, I'd convinced myself otherwise. God makes us wait at times so we can glean valuable lessons. But He never does so out of spite. This is something David taught me as I continued to wait for God to heal my husband.

Misconception #5: If I am waiting, I must not be working hard enough. We will look further into David's wait from the pasture to the palace in the upcoming chapters, but I want to remind you now of a significant point concerning David's kingship. David did not ask to be king. David did not dream of being king. He wasn't born into a royal family line from which he would naturally be appointed king. God chose David to be king. It is possible you and I could find ourselves waiting for something we never desired but God desires for us. He knows better than we do what we need to fulfill what He's called us to do.

> **Waiting well pushes through the pause**
> **by doing what we know to do.**

David had twenty years to work through his wait. Boy, did he work! Read his psalms to feel the agony of his wait as he cried out to God, "How long?" David worked hard, obeyed God, and ran from an enemy. His wait wasn't easy, but he pushed through the difficulties by doing what he knew to do: tend sheep, serve faithfully, and obey God patiently.

In each circumstance, these individuals sought God through prayer. They asked hard questions when they didn't understand His ways. We see that God may not have ended their waits, but He responded with loving faithfulness to all their needs.

FASTPASS, PLEASE

A few years ago, our family took a vacation to *the place where dreams come true*, Disney World. To prepare for the trip, I read websites and blogs and interviewed Disney World experts (aka, friends who call Disney World their favorite place on earth).

In my research, I discovered something called a FastPass, which is a printable ticket that gives you access to the most popular rides without having to wait in long lines. You get a ticket ahead of time, allowing you to go to the front of the line at an appointed time. It is ideal for girls like me who don't like to wait.

Each evening, my family would map out our ride plan. When the park opened the next morning, we would rush (notice that we rushed) to the FastPass machine. Our ride plan could not have worked out any better, but of course we were at Disney Word, where dreams come true.

Real life, though an adventure, is far from Disney World's Adventureland. Too often, we want a FastPass straight through God's pauses to move directly to His plan. God seldom hands out passes so you can avoid the wait and skip to the front of the line. That's not a bad thing, as painful as it is at the time. A rush through the wait has the potential to stunt our spiritual growth and dull our senses to what God wants us to learn as a result of our wait. As the apostle James tells us:

> Consider it a sheer gift, friends, when tests and challenges come at you from all sides. You know that under pressure, your faith-life is forced into the open and shows its true colors. So don't try to get out of anything prematurely. Let it do its work so you become mature and well-developed, not deficient in any way. (1:2–4 THE MESSAGE)

James advises those who follow Jesus not to take the FastPass through tests and challenges. He says that a pause will actually work in our favor. Our faith will mature, and we will become well-developed women of God, ready for all the good works He has prepared for us. God is the creator of time. We can trust His pauses to be purposeful and perfectly arranged. God will make the most of our pause, and we should too.

As "those who wait," we find ourselves in great company. Noah waited 120 years for the flood. Abraham and Sarah waited nearly a hundred years to become parents. Jesus waited thirty years to start His public ministry. These and countless others waited on God and in the wait experienced Him in remarkable and miraculous ways.

I know what you are thinking: *But he was Noah. They were Abraham and Sarah. And He was Jesus, the Messiah and Son of God. They are all in the Bible.* Rest assured, they are indeed all in the Bible, but not because of their perfection in waiting. All had moments when they questioned God. Not one was superhuman. They were men and women like you and me, but each was willing to wait and do the work necessary for God's plan to come to fulfillment.

Waiting isn't meant to be a grueling process. What if we view it as a pause or an interlude, a place we can experience the peace of God while He works in us so He can work through us? He is actively working while we wait—a promise that never disappoints in the end—and that work sometimes gets personal.

THIS PRINCIPLE IN THEIR PAUSE

Ashley easily became derailed from everyday life as she hurried to make sure everything was "just right" for her Bible study. She was sure of God's tug on her heart to teach and a bit confused when the class had to be canceled, but she realized she had rushed rather than rested in God's timing.

Samantha could have become entangled by the everyone-is-getting-married season of life. She asked herself the hard questions, prayed, and invited others to pray for her also. Samantha fought to keep the Person of her faith front and center in her wait.

Dianna waited for God to provide as she prayed. He proved faithful Jesus's words in Matthew 6:11, "Give us today our daily bread." Each day, her family had what they needed. She was fervent in her prayers, so why was God allowing things to be so hard? She wasn't opposed to the testing of her faith, but it seemed God was tightening the screws, and at times seemed unfair.

Our story: We started this health journey hopeful. *Scott will go to the doctor, get some medicine, and everything will be fine.* Our hope diminished quickly when the medicines were ineffective and Scott's condition worsened. Scott spent the better part of the year lost in the maze of various doctors who prescribed various medications. The ride left us weary and certain of one thing: our future was uncertain.

THIS PRINCIPLE IN YOUR PAUSE

Now it's your turn. Use the "Worth the Wait" pages in chapter 10 to examine your current wait in light of the lessons outlined in this chapter. Here are some prompts to help you get started:

Do I really believe that God is good and His blessings are not dependent on my "works"?

In what ways am I rushing through my wait? What *misconception* resonates most with me?

Misconception #1: I must not have heard God correctly.

Misconception #2: I must desire something not in God's will for my life.

Misconception #3: I must not be praying enough.

Misconception #4: I must not have enough faith.

Misconception #5: I must not be working hard enough.

Digging Deeper with David: Psalm 13

Read Psalm 13.

A wait doesn't sound terribly awful in the beginning. But as time passes, we become antsy and even question God about the length of our wait.

In the Principle in Your Pause section for the introduction, I asked you to write details about your current wait, including how long you have been waiting. Can we all agree that these are difficult seasons? Our emotions are up, down, and all around like an amusement park roller coaster. Spiritually speaking, we trust God one day and doubt Him the next. The "how longs" can even wear us down physically. This is where we find David.

It's undetermined when David wrote Psalm 13, but his words give us a snapshot of his circumstances. David, living in a *how long* season, was at his wit's end.

How many times did David ask God "how long"? _____

Can you hear the desperation in David's voice? Read verses 1–2 out loud for greater impact. I love that David asked these questions. Because he asked, you and I can feel the freedom to ask too.

LIVING "HOW LONG"

When I was a little girl, my daddy had a talk with my brother and me. "One day your momma will not be able to brush her hair and she will need help getting dressed. Her fingers will become crooked, making it difficult to do everyday, simple things. She has a disease called arthritis." I couldn't imagine this ever being a reality. My momma was a strong woman who loved the Lord and could do anything. And I knew God. He healed. And He would heal my momma. So at eight years old, I began to faithfully pray and believe that God would indeed heal my mother.

Like David, I tried to depend on God but sometimes cried out for answers. I was sure He could give this arthritis to someone else. There weren't immediate answers to my questions and cries, but leaning on God's strength made the "how long" bearable and my young faith stronger.

As our heavenly Father, God expects us to cry out to Him. He longs to lift the burden of our how long. The burden is lifted when we cast our cares and concerns on Him.

Read 1 Peter 5:7.

Why should we cast our cares on God? _____

What cares and anxieties of your current wait can you cast on God?

_____

_____

PRAYING IN "HOW LONG"

As the years passed, I never stopped praying for God to heal my mother. Praying made my young faith strong. Sadly, the longer I waited, the less I prayed. I remember being anxious, wondering why He was taking so long. Even through my anxiousness and wondering, it never occurred to me that He would choose not to heal her.

Despite his anxious heart, David's spiritual response to pray superseded his natural instinct to doubt. He directed his fretful and question-filled thoughts to God. David's natural instinct had become spiritual. He knew praying would, in time, bring peace of mind.

Read Philippians 4:6–7.

In what types of situations should we pray? What happens when we pray?

_____

_____

Through prayer, our natural instinct becomes spiritual. This transformation of thinking and responding enables us to dwell in our "how long" with hope for deliverance. Our response to this new hope is the impulse to praise. Yes, you can praise God in a season of waiting, no matter how long.

PRAISING IN "HOW LONG"

In just a few short verses, David's prayer changes from *how long* to *hallelujah*. Through prayer, David remembered God's past faithfulness, encouraging him to trust in God's future provision. Had his situation changed? Had his enemy suddenly decided to surrender? No. David was not delivered from the situation, but he was released from its despair. His anxiety was replaced with a new song of praise.

Read Psalm 40:3.

Who provided David with a new song? _____

As we pray, God will not only guard our mind and heart with peace, but He will also put a hymn of praise on our lips. Peace and praise produce endurance and unity with God, making a waiting period worthy of praise.

Are you living in the unbearable days of "how long"? Maybe like David you feel God has abandoned you. Praying and praising will not only make the long wait bearable, but they will also cause your faith to flourish. Your relationship with God will grow stronger even if your situation doesn't change.

Write verse 5 in the space below. Take a moment to read it aloud as a prayer to God.

_____

_____

We can trust God in our "how long" waiting period. He will sustain us until He is ready to deliver us. Oh, and we can be confident that our deliverance will be perfectly timed.

2

When Waiting Means Working Out

At six weeks old, Maxie came to live with us. After surveying all the puppies, we chose her and knew with great confidence she would be the perfect addition to our family. We had looked into her dark eyes and fallen in love. She displayed her love and appreciation to us by licking our chins and using her furry chocolate-brown paws to climb onto our laps.

Maxie's puppy days were full of running and retrieving. She was happy, except when she would spot her feathered nemesis in our front-yard tree. Being an energetic Boykin Spaniel, Maxie was very determined to get her bird. Boykins are bred to be bird dogs, so bird chasing is in her DNA. You might say it's her calling.

Every morning, Maxie robustly ran from her kennel to the tree. With her front paws propped on the trunk, she let out her loudest puppy bark as if to say, "Game on!" Getting no action, she would move just under the low-hanging branches and jump her highest puppy jump. This barking and jumping went on until Maxie finally gave up and panted her way back to the house. We knew she was thinking, *Oh, never mind. I'm too tired now anyway.*

We are a lot like Maxie. When God unleashes the dream in our heart, sets His plan for our life in motion, or stirs a hidden desire for something we know is possible only through Him, we can't wait to respond, "Yes, and how can I help?" Each day is spent going from place to place, doing this thing or that, trying to implement the plan. To make it happen, we run around, jump our highest, and put our gifts and talents to use. We spend hours researching, studying, and praying. I'm sure you get the picture. If we deplete ourselves trying to make our dream come true or purpose play out, we won't be ready when God runs His finger across the kingdom calendar and says, "Today is the day."

When that day comes, let's be ready rather than worn out. David is an excellent example of how to prepare while we wait for what God has planned for our lives.

GETTING READY

David has greatness in his lineage. He was the tenth generation in the line of Jacob's son Judah. One of his earliest ancestors crossed the Red Sea when Moses led the Israelites from Egypt. His great-grandfather was Boaz, a well-respected judge in Israel. But despite David's prestigious heritage, his family did not hold him in high esteem. Even though his father and brothers didn't recognize him, God did. He called David—who was just a boy at the time—a *man* after His own heart (1 Sam. 13:14). Perhaps this is one of the many reasons God sent the prophet Samuel to find David.

David was in the fields when Samuel came looking for the next king of Israel. He was simply doing his job when Samuel asked Jesse to call his youngest son. David was being faithful in the small things and obeying his father by tending to the sheep. He became a young man who loved and esteemed God by spending lots of time with Him in the hilly pastures of Bethlehem, gazing at His creation. The isolated meadowlands were David's classroom that prepared him to be king.

The anointing by Samuel happened in private. No fanfare. No parade. No proclamation of him being Israel's king. After David was anointed, he went back to his classroom, back to the place where he could do what he knew to do. Physically, he was unchanged; spiritually, he was altered forever.

DO WHAT WE KNOW TO DO

God does most of His work in us in private. He meets us in the pastures of life with a desire to cultivate within us a heart like His. This may take years, as it did with David. Often, we would rather rush through our time in the pasture than wait there to experience His work. Our inclination is to hurry to the finish line, when instead we should patiently stay put, showing ourselves faithful. How? By doing what we know to do and responding to our Father with obedience, even if it means staying in our pasture. Why? Because it's in the pasture that God is preparing us for what is ahead.

We have to allow God to do a work in us
before He can do a work through us.

In the early 2000s, I was minding my business when God introduced me to His plan to move me beyond my current pasture. I felt Him calling me to be a Bible teacher and active in women's ministry. Not really understanding what this meant or how to make it happen, I took my first step out of my current pasture and attended She Speaks, a conference geared toward women in ministry, hosted by Proverbs 31 Ministries.

In ways only God could arrange, this calling beyond my current pasture was confirmed. I was unsure what was involved in being a Bible teacher and Christian speaker, nor did I feel qualified. I wasn't even able to locate all the books of the Bible without the table of contents. *Should I go to seminary? How will Scott react to this calling? What if I misrepresent God's Word? Will I have to fly to different cities? I hate flying!*

Regardless of my insecurities, I was confident God wanted me to speak to women about Him and teach the truths in His Word. This new place of serving the Lord was on the horizon. However, in my typical high-speed fashion, with all my notes in hand, I returned home from the conference ready to get started. For weeks, I lived and breathed nothing but bio sheets, messages, headshots, and marketing.

> **My rush showed no regard for how God wanted**
> **to prepare me for what was next.**

I rushed to prepare myself for life beyond Pope Pastures. So you can imagine my surprise when my sprinting ahead did not result in calls for speaking engagements. My heart ached when my efforts accrued expenses that exceeded our family's budget. My rush showed no regard for how *God* wanted to prepare me for what was next.

Have you ever felt God calling you to something? How did you react? You could do one of two things: with good intentions, you could try everything in your power to fulfill the calling ... or you could wait for God to give you specific directions. There is wisdom in taking steps of action, *and* there is wisdom in waiting on God to tell you where to walk. It's all about finding the balance between the two. Think of waiting as controlled preparation, like getting ready to have a baby. Moms-to-be don't visit every pediatrician in their area several times a week or buy all the diapers on Amazon. Nor do they just sit at home waiting for the day of delivery. They take deliberate steps for months in anticipation of the big day. Mommas may change their diets to nourish their little ones and ask other mothers for wisdom. They definitely visit the doctor as necessary, buy maternity clothes, and pray (a lot!). As the due date for my firstborn crept closer and closer, my anxiety grew more and more. I organized and reorganized the nursery, drove the route to the hospital, and read *What to Expect When You're Expecting* until the cover was permanently folded over.

The same is true for God's timing and our preparation. Our job is not to run ahead of Him or lag behind. We should take natural, commonsense steps that are in line with His Word so we will be ready when He delivers our heart's desire. As we step out in faith, He will show us the way by either opening doors or closing them. Sometimes that will require we do a new thing, and sometimes it means doing what we already know to do.

A friend of mine wanted to write a book for ten years. Every time she got serious about starting the project, something deterred her: her family moved, she started a new job, she had another baby. God continued to close doors. A decade after He called her to write that book, she finally did. My friend realized the move, job, and baby each held lessons that ended up playing integral parts in her message. As she waited in her pasture—tending her sheep—God was getting her ready to share His heart in her book.

Waiting in the pasture and tending sheep are difficult when we feel God has called us to something different. Many of us Jesus girls are doers, created with a nature to fix, nurture, and make things happen. Therefore, we don't easily accept an assignment to hang out in our pasture and do the same old things when new things need to be done. And some of us Jesus girls are more cautious, created with timid hearts that seek confirmation.

Before we get discouraged or passive about hanging out on the hilly slopes of what we know, let's revisit James 1:4: "So don't try to get out of anything prematurely. Let [a test or challenge] do its work so you become mature and well-developed, not deficient in any way" (THE MESSAGE).

David was approximately ten years old when he was anointed king. He was not old enough or experienced enough to be king. Simply put, he wasn't ready for the throne. However, his time as a shepherd had prepared him to be king.

Like David's, our pasture experience will mature and develop us for the next season of life. Lingering in our field will teach us the trustworthiness of God and the vastness of His ways. If David had rushed to the palace, his kingship would have advanced quite differently. Yet if he hadn't taken the steps to get to the palace, he may never have been crowned. Who knows—we might never have been blessed by his poetic artistry of the Psalms. Regardless if we like it, it is necessary for Jesus's followers to embrace the pasture and tend to our sheep, as well as be willing to take a few steps toward leaving our current pasture.

Our pasture experience prepares us for what is next.

TENDING TO OUR SHEEP

David did what he knew to do in order to prepare for what he did not know. So what did he know? His primary responsibilities were to protect the sheep from predators, guide them to nutritious grazing, shear them, and monitor the lambing process. He did what he knew until God was ready for him to take the next step toward his kingship. He spent his days learning to recognize and obey God's voice, two traits that would serve him greatly as king. Sometimes our time in the pasture can be longer than expected, leaving us confused and wondering, *What should I do now?*

Do what you know to prepare for what you don't know.

In the apostle Paul's second missionary journey while preaching to the church in Philippi, he stirred up opposition when he cast an evil spirit from a young slave girl. This upset the girl's masters because they could no longer charge money for her fortune-telling services. Her masters had Paul and Silas brought before the magistrates for a public hearing, causing the crowd to rise up against them. The magistrates had them beaten and thrown into prison, but later they were miraculously set free (Acts 16:16–40). Despite this miracle by the Lord, the uprising threatened the growth of the young church. Members were paralyzed with the fear of persecution and the confusion of false teachings.

Paul had to move on with his mission work, but he didn't leave the young church hanging. While they waited and wondered what to do next, he wrote them a letter—what we now know as the book of Philippians—to instruct, encourage, and exhort them to remain faithful. They took his words to heart and supported Paul's missionary journeys, even when he was once again imprisoned. They showed compassion to the poor. This band of believers, perhaps without realizing it, tended to the sheep.

Let's examine one verse in Paul's letter to this church that will draw a line connecting pasture time, sheep tending, and doing what we know to do:

> Therefore, my dear friends, as you have always obeyed—not only in my presence, but now much more in my absence—continue to work out your salvation with fear and trembling. (Phil. 2:12)

Now let's circle our wagons around the phrase "work out your salvation." It is imperative we establish what Paul *was* and *was not* saying. Without clarification, we could easily find ourselves debating salvation by grace through faith in Jesus Christ with the idea of a works-based salvation (Eph. 2:8).

Paul said to "work *out* your salvation," not "work *for* your salvation." In no way did he suggest that salvation could be earned through doing good deeds. He was speaking to believers who had experienced the free gift of salvation through Jesus Christ. He encouraged them to demonstrate their salvation by doing what Scripture asks believers to do. Those who accept salvation witness a soul transformation. As a result of this transformation, obedience to God is birthed out of a desire to please Him rather than a duty to serve. This desire bids us to obey even when the instructions contradict natural inclinations.

Let's not miss the word *continue*. In simple terms, Paul encouraged the church to keep caring for the poor, nursing the sick, and staying true to what they knew. When our wait stirs within us the need to make things happen, we can become more preoccupied with moving forward than tending our sheep. We neglect working out our salvation. Our desire to end the wait is so overwhelming that we manipulate circumstances and design methods to make things turn out the way we want. Or worse, we try to make things happen the way we *presume* God wants them to turn out. This, my friend, is dangerous. The revered writer Oswald Chambers referred to individuals who conduct themselves in this manner as "amateur providences," people who attempt to make things happen. By injecting our actions and ideas, Chambers suggested we hinder God's progress as well as movement in our situation.

I acted as my own amateur providence when I rushed to accomplish everything I had learned at She Speaks. In a matter of weeks, I was raising my hand, saying, "Pick me! Pick me! I am ready to be your speaker." No one called. Remember Ashley, who also felt the call to be a Bible teacher? As I did, she thought she had it all figured out and jumped in with both feet. God wants us to step out in faith and follow His leading, but rest assured, He never rushes.

We have to stay in our pasture, doing what we know to do even if what we are doing isn't exciting or doesn't seem to be effective. Our soul is most satisfied and our life is most effective when we are where God wants us to be, doing what He wants us to do. Paul knew this, and that's why he encouraged the church at Philippi to stay put and "continue to work out [their] salvation with fear and trembling."

The Greek word used for "fear and trembling" is *trómos*.[2] This word describes the anxiety of one who completely distrusts his ability to meet all requirements but religiously does his utmost to fulfill his duty.[3] Let's not get tripped up on the word *religiously* and let it derail the impact of the power of the word *trómos*. In this context, *religiously* simply means "faithful."

Paul cautioned the church—and by extension, all believers—to trust and obey God. When we are waiting and wondering when things will come to pass, we should continue to do what we know to do. We have to trust that it is God who ultimately works things out, not our own abilities to make things happen. This goes against every fiber of our natural inclination, and we can stumble right over our own abilities when we don't wait on God to accomplish His work.

Remember my rush to become a speaker? I didn't trust God to initiate anything, so I struck out on my own. I worried, put my family in debt, and neglected my duties as a Christian. I was more concerned with accomplishing the goals of my plan than tending my sheep. Being preoccupied with writing the perfect bio sheet didn't give me much time for prayer, homework with my kids, or volunteering in my church. This can happen to any of us and is precisely why Paul told the Philippians to live with fear and trembling. This does not mean fearing hell or damnation. It is the righteous and awe-filled reverence for God every believer should have. It doesn't have to be the trembling of a guilty sinner; it should instead be the joyful trembling of an encounter with the glory of God, spurring us to do what we know to do.[4]

Even if it doesn't seem like it, God works while we wait.

WHAT DO WE KNOW?

We would be remiss if we did not ask ourselves, "What do we know to do?" David did what he knew to do when he returned to the pasture: he nurtured his sheep and his relationship with God. The church at Philippi went about what they knew to do: they worked out the things of their salvation.

What about you and me as we wait on the Lord? Each of us was made fearfully and wonderfully, unique to accomplish individual assignments. Maybe you are called to work in the neonatal intensive-care unit with critically ill babies while another person is called to serve in hospice care, assisting those in their final days on earth. Your place of service may be in a suburban home with a white picket fence, loving your husband and children. God may have placed you in the local library shelving books or in a high-rise making big decisions that will affect tomorrow's stock market. Perhaps you are a medical missionary or physician serving in a third-world country. Tending sheep in our own pasture is different for each of us. However, two things are the same for every believer.

When Jesus began His ministry, the teachers of the day made it their mission to trip Him up concerning the Law. Teachers in that era were called scribes, rabbis, and Pharisees. Their job was to make sure every Israelite was acquainted with the Law. One of these teachers asked Jesus, "Of all the commandments, which is the most important?" (Mark 12:28). This was a loaded question as these teachers were well versed in the Law. They were referring to the Torah, the first five books of the Bible, which contains 613 laws. But the teachers' knowledge was no match for Jesus, whose response answers our question, "What do we know to do?" He said:

"Love the Lord your God with all your heart and with all your soul and with all your mind and with all your strength." The second is this: "Love your neighbor as yourself." There is no commandment greater than these. (Mark 12:30–31)

Jesus clearly summed up what He wanted His followers to know and subsequently do: love God and love others. Simple yet complex, isn't it? Jesus used the word *love* to describe how we should treat God and others. Love is a verb. Love is an action. Love is demonstrated.

WE KNOW TO LOVE GOD

We demonstrate our love for God by spending time with Him and obeying what He asks us to do. I can think of no better things to do during our wait. In Mark 12:30–31, the word *love* in the Greek is *agapáō*. This means "to welcome, entertain, be fond of, and to love dearly." Take a moment to ponder the following questions as they relate to your love for God:

- Do I warmly invite Him into all areas of my life? (welcome)
- Do I keep and cherish Him in my mind? (entertain)
- Do I hold Him in the highest regard? (be fond of, love dearly)

If you answered a resounding *yes* to each of these, celebrate! If you struggled with your answers, you are not alone.

For years, I watched with envy *those* women who love God *that much*. You've seen them before; their glow seems to enter the room ahead of them. In Bible study or a small group, they confidently respond to a question or make inspiring comments concerning the lesson. It's as if they know God personally, on a first-name basis. *How do they know God and His Word like that?*

Tired of living with envy, I made a confession to God along with a request. *Lord, I confess I don't love You that much, like those other women. I want to love You that much. Will You teach me how?* This confession broke the dam that had been holding back my desire to know and love God.

With fear and trembling, I began to have a quiet time with God every day. I had no idea how to get to know and really love Him. For a long time, embarrassment and guilt were my companions. I was embarrassed because I had gone to church since infancy, yet I didn't really know God, and felt guilty because I didn't love Him *that much*. In the dark of the early morning, I would grab my Bible and sit in what I now affectionately call my "Jesus chair." Each day I read a psalm and prayed the same prayer: *God, help me know and love You.* After fifteen years of sitting in that chair, waiting and doing what I knew to do, I can say I love God *that much*. And if I can, you can too!

Waiting on God is a good time to solidify your love for Him. You can do so by getting to know Him through reading the Bible, studying His attributes, and journaling all the wonderful new things He teaches you. You will be amazed how your love for God spills over to others. It is only when we love God that we can truly love and have compassion for His people.

WE KNOW TO LOVE PEOPLE

Our love for others is generated from our love for God. It's easy to have blinders on when it comes to the cries of the less fortunate and sometimes even the cries of our family and friends. Life goes by fast, and most of us are really busy. Regardless, when we wait well, doing what we know becomes a priority. This means slowing down to notice and do something about the needs of others. As Jesus said, "By this everyone will know that you are my disciples, if you love one another" (John 13:35). The Greek word for *love* here is similar to the one used in Mark 12:30–31. *Love* in John 13 is the Greek word *agape*, which means "brotherly love, affection, good will, love, and benevolence." As our love for God grows, so will our love for others. Through Him, the desire to do good for others will become second nature.

Unless we are plugged in to our community or consistently attend a local church, it isn't always easy to see the needs of others. Once I became active in my church and got to know others, I found that loving God by loving people wasn't overwhelming. It wasn't just another thing on my to-do list. As we wait, God will reveal to us the people we can reach with His love. Showing love to others doesn't need to be complex.[5]

An underprivileged child needs school supplies; you purchase a book bag and fill it with provisions needed for a successful school year.

Do what you know to do. Work out your salvation.

A widow is unable to care for her lawn; you enlist volunteers (including yourself) to pitch in to do the work.

Do what you know to do. Work out your salvation.

A member of your church is unable to drive herself to Sunday services; you leave home early each week to give her a ride.

Do what you know to do. Work out your salvation.

A family in your neighborhood lost their home and all their belongings in a fire; you use your influence on social media outlets to generate assistance.

Do what you know to do. Work out your salvation.

When God places a burning in your heart for something new, it's frustrating to stay put and do what seems like the same old same old. Maybe your heart is aching for something different. You want to make it happen, but God sends you back to the pasture. Maybe you are fearful of making the wrong move or you aren't sure what God wants you to do.

Either way, we have to be ready when He says go. We have to be diligent to tend the sheep within our pasture. Let's work *out*, not *for*, our salvation by loving God and loving others. We can have peace to wait well, even though we don't know when He'll ask us to take the next step. Remember, God is a personal God. Spend time with Him as you hang out in your pasture and rest in His pause. The time you spend getting to know Him will help you recognize His voice and give you the confidence to obey His instructions, even if He asks you to move.

THIS PRINCIPLE IN THEIR PAUSE

Ashley could have let discouragement lead her to walk away from her calling to teach God's Word. She could have focused on other Bible studies offered in her church that hadn't been canceled (unlike hers) and become bitter. Instead, she turned her eyes back to the Person of her faith and submitted to follow wherever God would lead. He led her to start speaking to small groups, even some senior-adult groups.

Samantha got to know God better by studying His Word. As her love for God deepened, so did her love for others. She showed God's love by mentoring youth in her neighborhood and volunteering at an assisted-living home. Because she had previously served in similar capacities, these opportunities felt like a perfect fit. Much to her delight, Samantha found that when she was lonely or discouraged, loving God and others lifted her spirits. When her soul felt weary, serving refreshed her, just as Proverbs 11:25 says: "Whoever brings blessing will be enriched, and one who waters will himself be watered" (ESV).

Dianna waited for God to provide for her as she prayed. God confirmed that her new assignment was not to solve the problem but to love her husband. She helped her husband remain confident, secure, and wrapped in love as they waited for relief. As a result, he stayed the course, never wavering in his devotion to God or their family.

Our story: Scott continued in the saga of doctor appointments and medicines. The medicines took their toll on his mental health. The symptoms treated with one medication caused different physical health problems. My emotional health suffered as I watched him drift further from me and our life. I took care of our family while he struggled to stay present. We found small ways to love people in need and serve in our church, even though it was extremely difficult for us because we felt so discouraged.

THIS PRINCIPLE IN YOUR PAUSE

Now it's your turn. Use the "Worth the Wait" pages in chapter 10 to examine your current wait in light of the lessons outlined in this chapter. Here are some prompts to help you get started:

What steps am I currently taking to love God more?

How do I show love to others?

Are there ways I can do more for others while staying true to the pasture God has assigned me?

Digging Deeper with David: Psalm 16

Read Psalm 16.

Waiting and hanging out with God seems just fine if the waiting doesn't take too long. But we get fidgety when God requires us to stay in one place longer than we expect. It takes patience to stay in the same pasture when we know something greater awaits. David lived this truth with excellence.

From the moment of his anointing until the day he sat on his throne, David accepted God's boundaries. He stayed in the family pastures while playing the harp part time for King Saul. He accepted the borders of the palace when he moved there to work full time. He lived in the boundaries of caves and strongholds of the mountainous terrain as he ran when Saul threatened his life. David lived within his lines.

As with David, we can receive benefits, including portion control and security, when we live within the lines.

PORTION CONTROL

David was aware of god chasers. Just as it was prevalent in David's day, god chasing is a pastime for believers as well as nonbelievers in our day. When we are stuck in the same place for a long time and God doesn't seem to be paying attention to us, we can feel the urge to chase other gods.

My waits have been full of god chasing. Too often I abandoned the God with the big *G* for the god of the little *s*: shopping. If I felt lonely, I went to the mall. If I felt unloved or unnoticed, I went to Amazon.com. Chasing this god created a mountain of debt, which I tried to hide from my husband. Can I tell you a secret? You can't hide a mountain. It took many years before I could see the limitations and liabilities of god chasing.

David saw firsthand the trouble of god chasing. Consequently, he accepted his pleasant places and learned God was enough and provided enough. Everything that happened to David, good or bad, was portioned perfectly for him.

What happens when we run after other gods? (Ps. 16:4)

_____

What little gods are you currently chasing?

_____

Portion control provides contentment. David discovered that when God is all you've got, He is all you need.

SECURITY

God provides security as we live within the lines and guard the path toward the object of our wait. Since David was destined for the throne, sheep tending and cave dwelling could have caused him to doubt the fulfillment of this path. David's response demonstrates his confidence in God to make happen what He said would happen.

David wrote, "You make my lot secure" (Ps. 16:5). The word *secure* in Hebrew is *tamak*, which means "something used to hold or fasten a thing in place." Like a hook holds a picture securely on a wall, God has your future held securely in His hands.

Is it easy to completely trust God for the object of wait? Why or why not?

_____

_____

David talks further about the security God provides. Read Psalm 16:7.

What are the additional ways God provides security?

_____

_____

When the nights were long and the answers to life's concerns were short, David would seek God. And in the dark of night, God was faithful to provide the comfort David needed.

During the wait for Scott's health issues to be resolved, I learned and lived a verse that profoundly changed my heart toward God:

> Study this Book of Instruction continually. Meditate on it day and night so you will be sure to obey everything written in it. Only then will you prosper and succeed in all you do. (Josh. 1:8 NLT)

Take your pen and underline the words *day* and *night*. I won't lie. I loved the promise of prosperity and success, but these benefits were not my motivation for reading the Bible in the morning and night. Watching my husband suffer each day was heart wrenching. God's Word was my comfort in the storm of the wait. The company I kept brought me the peace I needed. He made my lot secure.

Is it difficult to stay within the lines of your life? Make a commitment to trust God to move the lines in His perfect time. Savor the benefits of the boundaries. Meditate on His Word day and night to experience His peace. And be confident that even if boundaries are rigid and painful, staying within the lines is the safest place to live.

David makes a vow in Psalm 16:8. I believe this is how he was able to maintain his confidence in God as he lived within the lines. Write David's vow in the space below.

_____

_____

Read it out loud as a prayer to God, replacing the pronoun *Him* with *you*.

3

When Waiting Gets Personal

I have never enjoyed exercise. Honestly, the thought of it makes me a bit nauseated. I truly admire those who are dedicated to their physical health and well-being. Over the years, I have tried to see working out as something fun—really, I have. But no program or regimen has driven me to dedication. Thankfully, I've found one regimen I can stomach and commit to regularly.

Though I am not a fan of exercise and would rather chow down some pizza with an ice-cold Dr Pepper five days a week, I walk two miles a day and treat myself to my favorite meal only once a week. Why? I know that a physical workout and healthy eating choices are good for me. We can choose to look at our pauses with God the same way. Though we may not necessarily enjoy times of waiting, they are good for us.

Travel back in time to a dark Carolina morning, and join me in my Jesus chair. As mentioned earlier, I had confessed to God that I did not love Him *that much* and asked Him to show me how to love Him more.

When God gets personal, we get the privilege
of knowing Him personally.

I just knew God was so proud I had finally confessed this personal problem that He would perform a water-into-wine miracle to fix everything wrong with the people who were hard for me to love. In addition, He would give a "peace, be still" command to my turbulent circumstances. Much to my disappointment, neither of these happened. Well, let me rephrase that. Much to my benefit, God didn't instantly change the people or hardships in my life. If He had, I wouldn't have known the joy of experiencing Him through truly dark times. You see, in our pauses, God gets personal. When God gets personal, we get the privilege of knowing Him personally.

GETTING PERSONAL CHANGES OUR HEART

God spoke startling words to Samuel the day he went to Jesse's home to anoint Israel's next king. Samuel was looking for a man who appeared to be kingly—tall, handsome, and confident. God responded to Samuel by saying,

> Don't judge by his appearance or height, for I have
> rejected him. The LORD doesn't see things the way
> you see them. People judge by outward appearance,
> but the LORD looks at the heart. (1 Sam. 16:7 NLT)

David's physical appearance at that time did not resemble a king, but his heart did. God could *see* his heart of obedience, kindness, gentleness, and humility. God could *see* David's heart to defend the weak from the powerful and violent. God sees your heart too. He sees our emotions, intellect, and desires. In fact, God was called *El Roi*, "the God who sees," by Hagar in Genesis 16:13.

God could see my heart as I curled up in my Jesus chair morning after morning. He saw my desperation to move from my waiting and wandering to a place of peace. But unlike David, I did not have a heart like God's. My heart *wanted* to be like His, but I had no idea how to *make* it like His. Fortunately, God knows exactly how to work with a want-to heart.

I thought my troubles, unhappiness, and lack of peace rested on the shoulders of the people and difficult circumstances in my life. It was their fault I didn't have a heart like God's and felt stuck in one wait after another. God met David in the pastures of Bethlehem to train him to be like Him. He met me in my home and tenderly began to reveal my heart and teach me how to have a heart like His. This is when and where He got personal.

WHAT ABOUT ME?

When we're focused only on ourselves, it's easy to wonder if God forgot about us. We want to ask Him if it will ever be our turn to "have it all." Underneath these questions is a heart that needs to get personal with the Lord. God gently revealed my heart's condition, but even truth revealed with tenderness is painful. These painful truths weren't heaped on me all in one morning as I sat in my Jesus chair. God acts with grace and mercy. In His timing, He disclosed what He saw—selfishness, bitterness, prejudice, and anger. In these moments of realization, I saw how my emotions were affecting those around me. For the first time, I began to think of someone other than myself.

Let me paint the picture for you. My two-year-old daughter didn't like to nap. I could hardly see over my very pregnant belly, and my husband owned his own business, which meant long hours away from home.

From my perspective, Scott enjoyed the luxury of eating out with grown-ups and traveling on a plane to other countries for work and often for pleasure. It appeared he breezed out of our home before trouble started and conveniently returned after the trouble had subsided. It seemed to me he had it made. My perspective was strongly skewed by a focus on *self*. Whether you are a single mom struggling to get by, a young executive on the corporate fast track, or working hard with your man trying to make ends meet, it's easy to get sucked into the "my life stinks" game and throw a pity party for one.

This self-focused mentality generated anger issues for me. I want to be clear: My anger wasn't a result of Scott being gone so much. His absence was the prompting God used to reveal a part of my heart that needed correction. Over time, anger poisoned my heart. Unfortunately, the only other person at home when my blood started to boil was my precious daughter. You remember her—the baby I had waited for through endless fertility trials and tests.

I was miserable, and I expressed it by being rude. Sarcasm and insults made me feel better, even if they were at the expense of my own child. But my uplifted mood never lasted longer than the day of my outburst. Looking back, I wonder if my daughter picked up her habit of throwing fits from her temperamental mom. Blaire could have been crowned Queen of Tantrums—at least, in my anger, it seemed that way. Because of her frequent tantrums, I came up with a horrible nick-name for her. Each time she would whine about something a toddler "shouldn't cry over," I would stare down into her innocent eyes and call her a terrible name. To this day, I am so ashamed that I can't utter the name aloud or find the fortitude to even type it.

This is not a story I tell often. Yet I want to share it with you because it's necessary to demonstrate the depravity of my heart—and the greatness of God's mercy and the depth of His love. Each time I press rewind and play this scene in my mind, my heart breaks all over again. The pain is as potent as if it just happened.

One day, the rustling of my daughter's diaper and slapping of her bare feet on the hardwood floors echoed as she ran through the house. I don't recall how things went wrong, but the happy swishing turned to sobs. Maybe a piece wouldn't fit properly in the puzzle or Tigger refused to bounce. What I do remember is not wanting to deal with a whiny two-year-old's tantrum.

She was crying, and I was stomping. Frustration got the better of both of us. In the midst of our own personal tantrums, my little angel responded to my anger for the first time. This is my earliest memory of God getting personal with me. He chose to reveal my heart through the sweet voice of my daughter. As with every other tantrum, I called her *the name*. Looking into my eyes, she said in bro-ken toddler talk, "Mommy, please don't call me that name." (Insert more mommy sobs.)

You're probably wondering, *How could she talk to her daughter that way? And she calls herself a Christian and a Bible teacher?* But maybe you can relate. It's easy to appear one way on the outside and feel totally different on the inside. We often fool others and even ourselves. Have you ever yelled at your kids all the way to church for making you late, then warmly shook hands with everyone in your Sunday school class? Or blown up at your spouse for not picking up his shoes, but wore a big smile for your dinner guests? Maybe you figured your family's negligence deserved your harsh reprimands. We frequently lack the self-awareness to see the depravity of our heart.

I stooped down to my daughter's level. My eyes brimmed with tears as I cupped her tiny face in my hands. "I'm so sorry. Mommy will never call you that name again." And I never have.

My anger did not totally dissipate in that moment, but I experienced God supplying the power I needed to change my ways. That day and many more to follow were difficult for me. However, that moment sparked the beginning of the end to my *what-about-me* mentality.

Because I was in a season of waiting, I was able to get personal with God. Waiting on Him is hard, but it softened my heart. For the first time, I could see the possibility of my heart resembling God's heart.

It's difficult yet necessary to admit we need to change. With each in-the-moment personal experience with God, we are drawn closer to His heart. It's the moment we choose not to listen to gossip about a coworker who got fired. It's the moment we could prove our rightness but choose to be silent instead. The closer we get *to* His heart, the further we get *from* sin. As God's work on our heart progresses, we eventually begin to see our new heart—the heart God sees—through the lens of redemption.

The closer we get to God's heart, the further we get from sin.

WHAT HE SEES

It's important to strike a balance when God begins to reveal our heart to us. We need to recognize our sin but also see the victory He offers. Otherwise we can get bogged down in shame, guilt, or defeat. In order to get a better understanding of what God sees when He looks at our heart, let's revisit 1 Samuel 16:7:

> The LORD doesn't see things the way you see them.
> People judge by outward appearance, but the LORD
> looks at the heart. (NLT)

Picture me leaning in, cupping my hand around my ear, and listening to the collective *hallelujah* we all are uttering as we read this verse. The Lord looks beyond flaws, failures, shortcomings, and all the things we tend to focus on in others. Like Samuel, we measure people by their exterior rather than the content of their heart.

Will you humor my inner word nerd for a moment? Let's examine the original Hebrew word *ra'ah* used for both *see* and *look* in 1 Samuel 16:7. It means "to see, look at, inspect, perceive, and consider." My favorite word in this definition is *inspect*. God carefully and critically looks at our heart. He loves us regardless of what we have done, are doing, or will do. He looks beyond our imperfections to see our potential. Oh, I love Him so!

Even though our heart is becoming more like His through the personal work we are allowing Him to do, it may still be difficult to see what He sees. The traits of our old heart and mistakes of our past cast shadows on the changes the Lord is performing.

Maybe you are like me and have allowed lies to distort the correct view of your heart. You may be thinking, *All this sounds good, but she hasn't lived my life.* You are right, but I have my own past full of pride, prejudices, pain, and other pollutants. We can't become discouraged. We must be determined to defeat discouragement with the truth.

I have a bay window in my kitchen that I love to look out when I'm cooking. Maxie does her bird-watching from that window and smears her nose prints on the glass. Much like the Windex I use to clean the window, we have to wipe our viewpoint clean with the truth so we can rightly see ourselves as God does. This is the best way I know to defeat despair.

The truth is the beginning of our freedom. Here's the truth about what God sees:

You See	God Sees	God Says
Failure	Victory	You are a conqueror (Rom. 8:37)
Endless	Temporary	Your circumstances are brief (2 Cor. 4:18)
Pain	Healing	You know the Lord who heals (Exod. 15:26)
Impossible	Potential	You are called to hope (Eph. 1:18)
Worthless	Valuable	You are fearfully and wonderfully made (Ps. 139:14)
Unaccepted	Accepted	You are welcomed by Christ (Rom. 15:7)
Ordinary	Special	You are created in His image (Gen. 1:26)

Poor	Rich	You have the riches of Christ (2 Cor. 8:9)
Unskilled	Gifted	You are gifted (Rom. 12:6)
Inferior	Superior	You have confidence (Heb. 10:35)
Guilty	Pardoned	You are forgiven (1 John 1:9)

It wasn't until I recognized my anger and the pain it caused my daughter that I saw my failure and guilt. That wasn't a pretty sight to see, trust me! But with God's truth, I could see past myself. Then I could embrace His victory over my temper and His forgiveness for my meanness. The freedom I received outweighed the discomfort and shame of acknowledging my old ways.

Is it easy to see the condition of our heart? Certainly not. However, the ongoing *pleasure* we enjoy in our relationship with the Lord far exceeds the temporary pain that accompanies getting personal with Him. His ongoing *presence* keeps our heart from the corruption of sin and prepares our mind for opportunities to be more like Him.

GETTING PERSONAL CHANGES OUR POSITION

Throughout His life, David chose God rather than self. He determined to keep his heart close to God's, where he could see and submit to opportunities that would be pleasing to God. In chapter 2, we talked about David's choice to go back to the pasture even though he had been anointed king. Yes, years before David ever wore the crown, he demonstrated a life of humility. Getting personal with God will lead to a change in our position too.

Here's an example from my life: One typical day I woke up not looking for a lesson in humility or expecting an encounter with the Lord. It was supposed to be a day filled with the simple pleasure of getting my hair cut. Maybe your simple pleasure is spending sunny spring days on the porch, drinking a fresh cup of coffee, or enjoying the company of a good friend over lunch. One of my favorite pleasures is a haircut.

My appointment was a week overdue, my roots were screaming, and I was eager to have my messy hair reshaped. Driving to the salon, I smiled as I imagined my stylist's fingers massaging my head as she shampooed and conditioned. Oh, the bliss!

After my cut, style, and primping, I grabbed my purse to pay for my new 'do. "Before I go," I said to my stylist, "I need to use your restroom."

Walking in, I immediately noticed the dirty ring around the toilet bowl, nasty stains in the sink, and, well, the gross things that form around the base of the commode. Disgusted, my thoughts turned to criticisms and questions about the sanitation regulations of the salon. In the midst of my mumblings, God got personal with me. I sensed the Holy Spirit whispering things I didn't want to hear.

"No. You can't be serious," I argued.

Again, He spoke. Again, I resisted. I found myself teetering. Would I follow the Holy Spirit's direction to clean that restroom or ignore Him and simply flush, wash, and leave?

Frozen, I could not move toward the door. My only option was to yield. I took a deep breath, grabbed a handful of paper towels, and obeyed the Spirit's direction. I wasn't thrilled or interested in doing a good job. I wanted to hurry and get out. In the lowly position on my hands and knees, scrubbing and wiping, the Holy Spirit nudged me. "Clean as if it's your own toilet."

It wasn't enough that I had obeyed and cleaned the bathroom. God wanted my heart to be right. So I cleaned with greater fervor, as if sanitizing my own home. As I worked to change the bathroom, the Lord changed me.

Waiting well demonstrates a willingness
to adjust our perspective.

UNDERSTANDING THE "H" WORD

C. S. Lewis wrote, "True humility is not thinking less of yourself; it is thinking of yourself less."[6] Many other authors have written about humility as well. Bible verses sing its praises. God desires it from us. Yet many of us don't readily embrace it. The truth is, opposing humility invites God's opposition. Scary thought, huh? The apostle James put it plainly: "God opposes the proud but gives grace to the humble" (James 4:6 NLT).

The Greek word for *oppose* is *antitassomai*, which means "to resist or be in battle against." Let's insert the definition in the verse: God *resists* or *goes to battle against* the proud. My resistance of God's call to be humble bids His resistance against me. *Whew!* I can hardly handle those words. While opposition comes against our pride, grace and kindness are lavished on our lives when we think more of others than ourselves.

Let's be honest—who enthusiastically volunteers to be last or longs to be the least? Who revels in the thought of their smallness? I most certainly did not want to clean the restroom in my hair salon, but my pride turned to humility as I thought about the next person who would use the facilities. As I shined the chrome faucet, I became more concerned with pleasing the Lord than the humble position I had taken by cleaning a public bathroom. The humility drew my heart close to God. David drew close to God as he cared for the sheep and carried food to his brothers on the front line of battle. As we wait on the Lord, we slow down and have time to learn lessons about humility we miss when we're busy trying to end our wait. Pleasing God one day compels us to please Him another day with a humble heart.

GETTING PERSONAL CHANGES OUR VIEW—ABOUT EVERYTHING

Thinking about yourself less is challenging at best. The closer we draw to God in our wait, the more capable we are for the challenge. Conquering selfish thoughts and behavior initiates a domino effect, and cooperating with God's work in our life starts with getting personal with Him. This nearness to the Lord leads to a softened heart. Humility transforms our mind-set from "what about me?" to "what about others?" As we take an interest in others, our wait becomes secondary. Naturally, this changes our view of the world.

> *Humility transforms our mind-set from "what about me?" to "what about others?"*

God's personal involvement in our life will expose sin, and this exposure disrupts our spirit. This spiritual disruption causes intolerance for the sinful things we used to enjoy; and instead, we long to be right with God. We begin to govern our choices to reflect His ways. As our heart becomes right with God, it is often wrong with the world.

SET APART

What images does the word *holiness* bring to mind? A cross? The Bible? Mother Teresa or Billy Graham? Maybe a better question to ask is what thoughts or emotions does the word *holiness* evoke? The word, as well as the concept, may make you think of personal reflection that will tempt you to breeze over this section. You might think, *I am not holy and never will be. There is no way I can be holy. Just look at the drugs I took, the abortion I had, the way I treated people, and all the sins I have committed.* If these are your initial thoughts, you're in good company. Even the apostle Paul felt this way. In 1 Timothy 1:15, he called himself the worst sinner of all!

Notice that the verbs in the italicized thoughts above are past tense. To some degree, we have all allowed our past to shape our future. Living as less than who God created us to be makes a mockery of who Christ died for us to be. It's vital that we believe we are holy! Why? Because God says so.

Being holy doesn't mean we are perfect. Being holy doesn't mean we are without sin. Being holy means that through God's mercy, and for a definite purpose, we have been set apart from those who don't know Him as their personal Savior. Noah was set apart or purposed to build the ark. Moses was purposed to rescue God's people from slavery and take them to the Promised Land. Mary was set apart to give birth to the One who would provide a way for you and me to spend eternity with God. And don't forget David, whose purpose was to be king of Israel.

Let's examine the darkness of our past-tense life in the life-giving light of Scripture. We can draw hope from a group of people called the Corinthians, with whom Paul established a church. Instead of sitting up and acting right, so to speak, the Corinthian people were world renowned for partying, drunkenness, and loose sexual morals. Their list of problems was a mile long; immorality and the abuse of doctrine, church government, spiritual gifts, church service, and authority ran rampant. The Corinthian church had a deserved reputation for the reckless pursuit of pleasure. It might be easy for us to think they weren't even saved! But they were.[7]

Paul wrote, "He made you holy by means of Christ Jesus" (1 Cor. 1:2 NLT). He was reminding the Corinthians of their heritage of holiness. He went on to say, "… just as He did for all people everywhere who call on the name of the Lord Jesus Christ, their Lord and ours." Did you notice the words *all people*? You and I are included in *all people*. According to Scripture, our holiness is not based on appearance or performance, but on Jesus's work on Calvary.

Paul drove this point home later in his letter to this fumbling church:

- "Christ made us right with God; he made us pure and holy, and he freed us from sin" (1 Cor. 1:30 NLT).
- "But you were cleansed; you were made holy; you were made right with God by calling on the name of the Lord Jesus Christ and by the Spirit of our God" (1 Cor. 6:11 NLT).

The Corinthians were invited and welcomed into God's family, despite their unruly past. Like them, we cannot do anything that will disqualify us from holiness. We are set apart and sealed with the holiness of God when we accept Christ as our Savior. The initial declaration of holiness is all about our position with God as His children. However, as we get to know God and yield to His leadership, our holiness progresses and our faith grows. This is a participatory process. God declared us holy based on our belief of His truth and acceptance of His Son as our Savior, but He will not control us like a puppet. The degree to which our holiness progresses is based on our participation with the Holy Spirit's work in our life.

The "set apart" mentality works in tandem with the Holy Spirit. Together, our mind-set and the Spirit empower us to make the hard decisions necessary to ensure progress in holiness. This happens each time we choose God's way instead of our way. Growing our love for God as we wait is a wonderful motivator to obey Him. When we do, we can deposit that victory in our spiritual bank and make a withdrawal the next time we face a "set apart" decision. The choice may concern a certain book to read, a place to visit, a relationship to maintain, or in my case, a television show to watch.

By the start of my "set apart" training, I had been watching a certain 10:00 p.m. television drama for many months. At first, the show's story lines portrayed fairly innocent adult situations and humor. But as the seasons progressed, the situations became increasingly lewd, moving more scenes from the living room to the bedroom. My heart and mind became unsettled. I knew the Spirit was gently counseling me to change the channel. Yet I leaned on my own understanding and ignored His warning. I told myself, *The show isn't that bad. It isn't as immoral as that show on that other channel. No one is watching it with me. How bad can it be?*

My beloved television program coincided with a Bible study I was leading at the time. Participants were encouraged to give up something for six weeks. Pretending to be a good Bible study girl, I committed to turn the channel at 10:00 p.m. Let me tell you, I was so proud of myself. Yes, indeed. I could effortlessly change the channel. Easy peasy. No sweat. How? Because I had set the show to record on a weekly basis. You can be sure that I planned to watch every episode I was giving up at the end of those six weeks. (I know—it sickens me too.) What a mockery I made of God's call to holiness and being set apart.

It wasn't until the conclusion of the six weeks that I felt the impact of my subversive recording. As I turned on the VCR (this was a while ago!) to watch the missed shows, I felt physically ill and spiritually nauseated as I heard the theme song. Without hesitation, I ejected the tape and threw it in the trash. To this day, I haven't watched the show. (God said no to reruns too.)

When God prompts us to say no to something, we can trust that it is for our good and His glory. It may not be easy or even make sense at the time. But rest assured, our call to holiness is the path to God's peace as we wait for His plan.

STAY STEADFAST

David remained humble, even after Samuel anointed him with oil. He demonstrated humility by going back to the pasture to do what he knew until he knew something else to do. The pastures of Bethlehem were the perfect classroom to make his heart soft and his character strong. The physical anointing of oil was a symbolic representation that he was set apart to accomplish a great purpose; however, the oil was only a symbol. Like you and me, David had to grant God access to his heart to cultivate holiness. David was ready to move toward his future as king of Israel only because he allowed God to work in his present.

We often interpret our seasons of wait as inconvenient, an interruption on the way to the ultimate outcome. Might I suggest we view our wait as an intermission rather than an interruption? It's kind of like an intermission in a really long movie, although I'm not suggesting a wait is a time of fun with popcorn, pretzels, and a giant Icee.

My mom, daughter, and bestie and her momma watched the three-and-a-half-hour drama *The Sound of Music* in the movie theater. As the word *intermission* rose to center screen, I felt relief. Don't get me wrong, I love the movie, but I had been sitting so long that I was getting fidgety. Plus I really needed to use the ladies' room. The intermission gave me the opportunity to refresh myself and pause my thinking. It was exactly what I needed to stay focused and engaged with the rest of the movie. Sometimes God's greatest work happens during intermission.

Maggie experienced an intermission when her husband, James, asked their oldest son to leave their home. They prayed that their son would become a godly man, work hard for honest wages, and someday lead a family of his own. But Caleb had a different idea about how his life would be, and he wanted to live by his terms. Though his parents offered grace and godly guidance, Caleb refused to obey their guidelines. As the head of their home, James told his son he could no longer live there. With a broken heart, Maggie supported her husband's leadership and watched her son pack his bags. Her intermission started the day the locks were changed.

As she waited, she focused on the Person of her faith. Maggie invested time in young women in her church by teaching a class on biblical marriage. As she grew her relationship with God, her commitment to pray for Caleb never waned. For five years, she prayed. For five years, she waited. For five years, she carried his Bible in her purse.

Maggie used her intermission as a time of refreshing and connecting with the Lord. Because she determined not to view her wait as an interruption, she could fully engage in a renewed relationship with her son when, out of the blue, she received the text that said, "I've packed my bags. I'm ready to come home and follow the Lord."

Though waiting can often feel like a placeholder we impatiently long to be done with, it is beneficial. We get to know God, love Him and others more, and grow in humility and holiness. By not giving up and letting God determine the how and when, we experience divine encounters with Him we might otherwise miss.

THIS PRINCIPLE IN THEIR PAUSE

Ashley achieved great results in her work life. But teaching Bible study didn't come as easily as she had pictured in her mind. It was *hard* to step out in faith. Women didn't rush to sign up for her Bible study just because it was listed in the Sunday bulletin and posted on the church website. Cancellation of her study humbled her to her knees. She asked God to search her heart and uncover her self-centeredness. She realized she had sought to lead the Bible study and obey God in her own strength. Ministering to women would require continuous humility and obeying God in His strength. She learned to remain willing, stay humble, and keep watching for God to reveal Himself through each part of the journey.

Samantha knew her questions of "how long?" and "why not now?" could drive her nuts. To take her mind off herself, she invested in other marriages by babysitting for couples. As she did, she prayed for the kids and their parents, which connected her heart with the Lord's. Samantha began asking the Lord to help her (and her future husband) live out the verse "He has told you, O man, what is good; and what does the LORD require of you but to do justice, and to love kindness, and to walk humbly with your God?" (Mic. 6:8 ESV). This helped her put aside her desires and focus instead on doing God's will.

Dianna says that the wait tried to strip her of dignity but God used it as a way of removing superficial compassion and replacing it with His heart. It was an aspect of Christlikeness she might not have developed otherwise. Dianna clung to the verse in Matthew 25: "And the King will answer them, 'Truly, I say to you, as you did it to one of the least of these my brothers, you did it to me'" (v. 40 ESV). She says, "God became such a part of our family during those days that I felt like I should have set a plate for Him at dinnertime."

Our story: God definitely got personal with me. For the most part, Scott turned away, not wanting to be personal with a God who wouldn't respond to his desperate pleas for answers. But the still, small voice of the Holy Spirit was whispering to a part of Scott's heart that he had kept closed from God, the self-reliant part that said, "I can take care of things myself." Scott slowly began to realize he had to rely on God to be the navigator of his wait.

THIS PRINCIPLE IN YOUR PAUSE

Now it's your turn. Use the "Worth the Wait" pages in chapter 10 to examine your current wait in light of the lessons outlined in this chapter. Start by praying the following verses from Psalm 139 (THE MESSAGE):

> GOD, investigate my life;
>> get all the facts firsthand.
> I'm an open book to you;
>> even from a distance, you know what I'm
>>> thinking. (vv. 1–2)

> Investigate my life, O God,
>> find out everything about me;
> Cross-examine and test me,
>> get a clear picture of what I'm about;
> See for yourself whether I've done anything
>>> wrong—
>> then guide me on the road to eternal life.
>>> (vv. 23–24)

Here are some prompts to help you get started:

How can you make your heart soft toward God's work in your life?

In what ways is He changing your heart?

How is He teaching you humility?

Digging Deeper with David: Psalm 40

Read Psalm 40.

David waited—and not always in the green pasture of rolling hills or the harpist's room of a plush palace. Sometimes he waited in a muddy mess. Scripture doesn't give the date of this occasion or let us know if David was in an actual dungeon, cistern, or grave when he penned Psalm 40. Whether David's place of captivity was figurative or literal, there is no doubt he had to wait to be rescued. He called this place a pit.

DEFINING PIT

David was able to wait well because of his intimate relationship with God. The genesis of his intimacy can be traced back to the day of his anointing, but the depth of the relationship was a result of David's cooperation with the Spirit's work in his life. As Samuel poured the oil, the Spirit of the Lord came upon David (1 Sam. 16:13). David lived life relying on the Spirit of God to guide and rescue him, and every trial he endured drew him closer to God. You might say David's godly character was shaped by every *p*ersonally *i*ntense *t*rial (PIT) he experienced.

Our waits are full of PITs. How much more enjoyable would our wait experience be if we saw our PIT as a reset rather than a setback?

ADJUSTING OUR PERSPECTIVE OF A PIT

I get it. We want our wait to be over, *and* we want to have thriving intimacy with God. We have to believe that despite our feelings of abandonment our wait is in the perfect and capable hands of a God who loves us very much. His desire is to use every experience we have, including PITs, to make us more like Him. And He is trustworthy to make everything work out in our favor. He's just that kind of God!

Adjustment #1: Believe God Loves Me Even If My Feelings Tell Me Something Else

Read John 3:16 and Romans 5:8.

In light of these verses, how did God demonstrate His love for you?

_____

God sent His Son to die for "*whosoever.*" We give Satan victory when we believe anything less. Repeat after me: "I am a 'whosoever,' and God loved me so much that He sent His Son to die so I could live eternally with Him." (Repeat as often as needed.) Satan deserves defeat, not victory.

Adjustment #2: Moving from My PIT and toward the Object of My Wait Is Not All on God

Read Romans 8:28.

Write out the verse in the space below.

_____

_____

For most of my life, I focused on and recited only the first part of this verse—the everything-will-work-out-for-my-good part. It was only a few years ago that I realized the for-my-good part had a participation clause. Underline the word *who* and the remaining words in the verse.

What is our role in *all things working for our good*?

_____

The first part of the verse is directly related to the last part of the verse. Those who love God and are called according to His purpose will see all things work together for good. We have to take action so God can take action.

Our action is to love God and conduct ourselves in a manner that reflects His purposes. As our perspective changes, the intensity of our personal trial and the object of our wait pale in comparison to pleasing God. This adjustment could revolutionize our relationship with God!

Adjustment #3: Every PIT Can Be Beneficial

Read James 1:3.

What does our PIT produce?

_____

As in David's trial, if we cooperate with the Spirit's work and live our life to please God, we can easily view our personal trial as a reset, not a setback. James, the brother of Jesus, teaches that the testing of our faith produces perseverance. Let's take a closer look at the word *perseverance*: "steady persistence in a course of action, a purpose in spite of difficulties, obstacles, or discouragement."

Steady says we can't stop even if the progress is slow. We keep on keeping on. This isn't easy, I know. When the going gets hard, we want to just give up. *Never mind. I don't care anymore.* The problem with this thought is that we *do* still care. Oh, the benefits of perseverance!

Read Romans 5:4.

What attributes does perseverance produce?

_____

Perseverance doesn't sound so bad after all, does it? Staying the course and working through our personal trials while we wait gives us hope. Now I ask, who doesn't want a little hope to hold on to?

Adjustment #4: God Is Never Inactive While I Wait

Though it might seem God has abandoned us or turned away while we suffer through our PIT, nothing can be further from the truth. Let this truth set you free. As we read in John 5:17, "My Father is always working, and so am I" (NLT). God the Father, the Holy Spirit, and Jesus are always at work. God's work is always good. We can take that to the bank and trust God as He moves us toward the object of our wait.

4

When Waiting Means Moving

I am a self-proclaimed creature of habit and avoid change if at all possible. This lifestyle offers me a sense of security. There's no guesswork in my schedule because my routine has remained the same for decades. Shopping is easy because I know what I am going to buy and don't get sidetracked by new brands. Eating out is simple. I never have to wonder if my dinner will be good. Of course it will! I eat the same entrée each time I go. Can you identify?

Does your sense of security flee when you hear the word *change*? Regardless if you're a creature of habit, there is a certain comfort in consistency. When change occurs, our comfort in the same old same old is replaced with skepticism. This skepticism then evokes fear and trepidation that cause us to pull the covers over our head, place our fingers in our ears, and sing a happy tune of "La la la la la la."

***Step out of the security of the familiar to
find peace in the unfamiliar.***

SOMETHING DIFFERENT

While avoiding change can make us feel like we're in control, we won't be able to maintain a tight grip forever. Take it from someone who has lived in the false sense of security of *same*: *different* is not all that bad. We just have to adjust our perspective and *surrender* to God's will and plan. Surrendering promotes peace, while staying the same creates complacency.

God wants to take us to new places and do new things in our life. Different may look like a desert of impossibilities with no direct route to the object of our wait, but God desires to make streams in our deserts and pave a way in our wastelands (Isa. 43:18–19). As we *surrender* to His ways, we prepare our heart to accept and embrace change. Peace begins to release the white-knuckled grip we have on our comfort. Peace transcends our understanding while guarding our heart and mind (Phil. 4:7). Peace girds us with confidence to step away from the security of the same and provide courage to move on to something new.

Earlier, I shared how God called me to a life of ministry. What I didn't tell you was where He called me. After I rushed to prepare my messages, hurried to pose for pictures, and scurried to build a website, God moved me to an office chair in a gray cubicle at Proverbs 31 Ministries (P31). There was not a pulpit or platform anywhere near my new three-by-three-foot "pasture." My mind raced with questions. *Did I hear God wrong? Why am I working in an office instead of teaching His Word?* Over the next few months, I learned the answer. Sometimes the next season of the wait is (insert deep breath) another wait.

WAIT, WHAT?

It's true. One wait often leads to another. That's the not-so-good news. The so-good news is that God works where He sends us to wait. Let's step back to the sunny slopes of Bethlehem's hillside and find out what God did during David's wait.

David didn't think twice about rejoining his sheep after being anointed king. Working as a shepherd in the quiet pastures gave young David ample time to *know* God. Waiting forces us to be still. When we are still, we get to *know* God as the young shepherd boy knew God.

Regardless if we like it, waiting is advantageous to our journey and offers a huge benefit, as we see in Psalm 46:10: "Be still, and know that I am God."

What does it mean to really *know* God? How does one get to *know* a holy God? The word nerd in me must share! There are roughly 800,000 words in the Bible. *Know* easily rises to the top as one of my favorites. *Know*, or *yada*, means "to perceive, discern, discriminate, distinguish, recognize," and (drumroll, please) "know through experience." We can sum up the definition in one word: *experience*. We have to *be still* so we might *experience* God.

How cool would it be if David had authored Psalm 46? While he had vast amounts of time to be still and experience God, he didn't write this particular psalm. The descendants of Korah penned these powerful, challenging words.

David wasn't privileged to have the whole Bible to read and study. There wasn't a church on every corner of Bethlehem with preachers or speakers teaching how to have a closer walk with God. David had

God to help him experience God. That is a sobering thought, isn't it? *Would I know God if all I had was God?*

We learn to recognize God's voice through our experiences of trusting Him as our provider and teacher, protector and healer, and confidential friend. Our experiences build a faith strong enough to courageously overcome our fear of change and accept our call to move.

OBEY OR DELAY

Come sit beside me in my little gray cubicle. I assure you, this is not where I thought I'd be after I surrendered. I believed saying yes to God would put me center stage in an arena filled with thousands of women who had just read my bestseller. Oh, my vanity!

Instead, God placed me in an office. My job? To write thank-you notes to P31 donors, maintain relationships with monthly partners, and code bills. For ten years I sat at my desk, stuffing envelopes and filling in spreadsheets. As I dutifully obeyed God and waited for the next move in my ministry, I experienced His peace, goodness, and joy. Want to hear something ironic? Neither center stage nor a bestseller matters to me any longer.

Surrender draws you nearer to the Person of your faith. Mysteriously, the thing we are waiting on becomes secondary or even further down the line of importance.

When God calls, do we delay or start on our way?

Shifting the focus from *my* plans to *God's* plans required faith. I had to accept the possibility that an up-front teaching ministry wasn't in God's plans for me. This step became easier when I focused on God, not ministry. Likewise, David stayed near the Lord. As a result, he confidently moved from the family pastures to the palace floor. God finally gave David the green light to change his address to the palace, but not to be king. His new role included serving the current king, Saul, as a musician. It turned out that Saul had disobeyed God in a battle with the Amalekites, and God had replaced His Spirit in Saul with one of torment and distress. As we read in 1 Samuel, Saul was troubled and irritated. His servants noticed his anxiety and offered a possible solution: "Let our lord command his servants here to search for someone who can play the lyre" (16:16). Saul agreed that a skilled musician might soothe his troubled soul.

David proved to be the perfect person for the job. He served his earthly father well, demonstrating loyalty and dependability. His days in the pasture prepared him for his service in the palace. As an accomplished composer and harpist, David pleased King Saul. His trustworthiness and obedience to authority put him in good standing with the royal court. When Jesse called him from the field, without any questions or delay, young David took a donkey loaded with wine and bread and followed Saul's servant to Israel.

Fresh from the sheep pasture, and well prepared, David wasn't ready to be king. However, he was ready for a new classroom, a new pasture, to learn how to effectively rule his kingdom. God knew this and placed him in the best position to learn as he waited a while longer to take his rightful throne.

David's pause in the pasture was the way God prepared him for his next pause. God doesn't map out His plan for us in a colorful PowerPoint presentation. Often we become frustrated in our pause, then when God says move forward, we hold back because things don't look how we think they should. Certainly, David didn't expect his move to the palace would be another service job. With God, different isn't bad. Different is exciting and gives us the opportunity to know Him experientially as He prepares us for greater things.

God never wastes a minute of our wait, and neither should we. David made the most of his days in the pasture. So when God told him to move, he felt ready and confident to obey without delay. We don't see any mention in Scripture where David complained about serving once he moved to the palace. He never manipulated the situation to strong-arm his way to the throne. He simply did the next thing.

DO THE NEXT THING

It sounds exciting to "do the next thing" when that next thing is interesting. But if we can't put the pieces of the puzzle together, we may scratch our head and wonder, *How is this drawing me closer to the object of my wait?* Instead, we should evaluate how the wait is drawing us closer to the Person of our faith.

Serving in the gray cubicle—though a head-scratcher—seemed to be my next thing. God's purpose for placing me in a position to work with numbers escaped me. I couldn't even balance my own checkbook. Writing letters and notes wasn't my thing either. *Why am I not out there speaking and growing my ministry?* I wish I would have had a good, biblically sound answer for that frustrated woman, but I didn't. Knowing what I know now, experiencing all that I have experienced, my simple response is this: do the next thing until God says you are ready to move forward.

WHAT KEEPS US FROM MOVING FORWARD

God planned all along for David to be king. He knew every experience needed to prepare David for the throne. You and I can be sure God has a plan for each of us too. We can trust Him to complete the plan, even if we are redirected and taken on a different course than we expected.

Let's have some fun and climb aboard a time-travel machine. After buckling up, turn the dial to the period surrounding Egypt's eighteenth-century dynasty, around 1513 BC, 480 years prior to the building of Solomon's temple.[8]

God has seen the suffering of His beloved Israel at the hands of the Egyptian ruler, Pharaoh. He declares now as the time of rescue from slavery and selects Moses, a descendant of Levi, to rescue His people. After a series of dramatic plagues, such as water turning to blood and locusts consuming all the crops, Pharaoh agrees to let God's people go. (Pause to lean in close. I am singing a jamming rendition of "Pharaoh, Pharaoh, whoa, whoa, let my people go" with a huge emphasis on the "whoa, whoa." End pause.)

In our adventures with God, we should expect the unexpected.

After more than four hundred years of watching His people be mistreated, you'd think God would send them on the fastest track away from Egypt to the Promised Land He had waiting for them. He didn't. God knew the Israelites' strengths and weaknesses and could foresee the best route for them to take. In our adventures with God, we should expect the unexpected. So here's what happened:

> When Pharaoh finally let the people go, God
> did not lead them along the main road that runs
> through Philistine territory, even though that was
> the shortest route to the Promised Land. God said,
> "If the people are faced with a battle, they might
> change their minds and return to Egypt." So God
> led them in a roundabout way through the wilder-
> ness toward the Red Sea. (Exod. 13:17–18 NLT)

Zero in on the phrases "did not lead," "even though," "the short-est route," and "might change their minds." God's people had a long history of war with the Philistines. Even though the Egyptian regime was cruel, God knew if they faced an enemy from their past they would run back to the familiarity of Pharaoh's harsh rule because they were too weak to battle with an old adversary. Their fear of Pharaoh was greater than their faith in God. Knowing their weak-ness, God took them on a faith-building field trip.

Let's be honest—if given the choice, we would all choose the short-est route to the object of our wait. Even though we know God wants to do a new thing, we prefer the fast track with the least resistance. But God, knowing our weaknesses and vulnerability, often chooses to lead us via a longer route so we can learn to trust Him more.

We hesitate to embrace the next thing and move forward. God knows that. Even as we're surrendering, we vacillate with uncertainty. *Can I really trust God?* The *what ifs* become louder and louder. He knows our fears, doubts, and hesitations. He knows a *longer route* (aka, our *next thing*) will provide opportunities to experience Him and resolve our moving-forward issues. He uses our *next thing* to build a faith bank of trust. Consider five common obstacles we might encounter while waiting it out on our longer route.

Obstacle #1: We Waver

God said, "They might change their minds." When the wait is long or filled with obstacles, the temptation comes to bail out and stop following God. He knew the Israelites would falter and change their minds if confronted with battle. How about you? What deters you from waiting on God and following His route for your life? For me, it's wavering thoughts. One day, I am fully convinced of God's ability to bring me through my wait; the next day, I wonder if the wait will ever end. On Monday, I am confident that I heard God correctly; come Friday, I am full of doubt. Back and forth, back and forth. I bounce between resting and wondering.

I could write a book about the trouble my reasoning has gotten me into over my lifetime. Thankfully, Proverbs 3:5 has revolutionized my thought process: "Trust in the LORD with all your heart and lean not on your own understanding."

Grab a highlighter. Press the tip of the marker in front of the *l* in *lean* and drag to the right until you have covered the *g* in *understanding*. This has become my waver mantra. Each time a restless, doubtful, or negative thought tries to creep into my mind, I simply pray, "Lord, I know You understand all aspects of this situation and You are in control. Help me not to lean on my understanding, but to trust Yours."

Each day provides a myriad of opportunities to lean on God's understanding rather than our own. Personally, I have always been a little too confident in my own understanding, and this confidence has led to impulsive decisions. My knee-jerk reactions have disrupted God's work. The disruptions have made my stay in the waiting place longer than necessary.

As I moved from pasture to pasture, I learned to apply God's Word to my situations. For example, when my husband needs my help, I get up and help him. This might sound simple, but hang in there with me. Basically, my nature is selfish. If I am comfortable or doing something I enjoy, I don't want to help anyone, not even the man I love. (Sorry if that disappoints you, but I'm trying to keep it real.) God designed me to be Scott's helper. As I embrace my role, I demonstrate to God my readiness to move forward in His plan. The more we learn about God and His ways, the more we understand God. The more we understand God, the less likely we are to ever lean on our own understanding. This leaning empowers us to end the vacillating thoughts about waiting that seek to steal our peace.

Obstacle #2: We Fear

When we let our thoughts run outside the boundaries of Scripture, we begin to fear. As I see it, fear can be summed up in two words: *the unknown.* Holocaust survivor Corrie ten Boom had a front-row seat to fear and its companion, waiting. Her words can bring us great encouragement as we learn to triumph over the paralyzing power the unknown can induce. Corrie wrote, "Never be afraid to trust an unknown future to a known God."

What about this known God? Here's what He says about fear: "So do not fear, for I am with you; do not be dismayed, for I am your God. I will strengthen you and help you; I will uphold you with my righteous right hand" (Isa. 41:10). If you have a pen handy, underline the words *righteous right hand* and hang on for some really good stuff. A few verses later, we read, "For I am the LORD your God who takes hold of your right hand and says to you, Do not fear; I will help you" (Isa. 41:13). Also underline *right hand* in that verse.

It's unnatural and awkward to hold a person's right hand with your right hand unless you are standing face to face. Can we close our eyes, take a deep breath, and picture our known God standing face to face with us in our unknown? Holding our right hand with His righteous right hand, He whispers, "I've got this. Don't worry." How much easier would our longer route be if we pictured this when fear creeps into our thoughts?

Obstacle #3: We Lack Confidence

For too long, I allowed doubt to dwarf my confidence. I wondered, *How can I be a good wife to Scott and mother to my babies? I fail at everything. Nothing ever goes right for me.* God inspired numerous verses about confidence to be recorded in Scripture, such as: "So do not throw away your confidence; it will be richly rewarded. You need to persevere so that when you have done the will of God, you will receive what he has promised" (Heb. 10:35–36).

In my wildest imagination, I could not think of one reason why God would use me for His glory. Have you struggled with doubt and insecurity too? It might very well be that God is establishing the confidence necessary for His plan as we are doing the next thing. We need to give God time to develop our confidence in Him and in the abilities He has instilled in us.

While we need to have confidence in the Lord, we have to guard ourselves from going overboard with it. Sometimes confidence forgets its generator. We finally get the promotion we've worked hard for and pat ourselves on the back for a job well done. Or after years of parenting, our kids grow into good workers, caring spouses, and loving Christians, and we accept all the praise. Let's be careful not to trip over our flesh and forget our source: "For the LORD will be your confidence, and will keep your foot from being caught" (Prov. 3:26 NKJV).

Obstacle #4: We Consider Self

You don't have to teach people to consider themselves. If you have any doubt, spend some time around toddlers. About the time those precious chubby legs learn to walk, their instinct of "mine" is exposed. Shortly after conquering the words *momma* and *dada*, the four-letter word *mine* rolls from their innocent lips. What's revealed at eighteen months takes a lifetime to defeat.

As I sat in my gray cubicle, a severe case of the "mines" attacked my heart. Near the same time, many of my friends in ministry enjoyed success. Publishing opportunities, consistent speaking engagements, and individual ministries seemed to fall into their laps, but not mine. I pasted on a halfhearted smile when they shared about their ministry growth, but inwardly I pouted and argued with God. *What about me? I've been speaking longer than she has. When will my ministry grow? Why can't my book be published?*

Don't get me wrong—I loved these precious women of God and hated feeling that way. In a meeting at P31, we were celebrating the growth of the ministry and the achievements of people on staff. As I waited for someone to ask about the growth of my online teaching ministry, jealousy welled up within me. No one asked. My heart pounded like a drum in a marching band. I couldn't wait for the meeting to be over. My view of self was so distorted. God planned to leave my feet planted firmly in the pasture of office work until I could learn to truly celebrate others' successes.

James, one of Jesus's brothers, gives some strong warnings about focusing on mine, mine, mine: "But if you harbor bitter envy and selfish ambition in your hearts, do not boast about it or deny the truth. Such 'wisdom' does not come down from heaven but is earthly, unspiritual, demonic. For where you have envy and selfish ambition, there you find disorder and every evil practice" (James 3:14–16).

King David certainly had every opportunity to boil with envy. Saul sat in "his seat" and ruled the country he was ordained to rule. Yet David did not respond with envy, disorder, and evil. He simply served and did so with joy. I have so much to learn from David!

Obstacle #5: We Don't Believe

Let's dash back to Egypt's open gates as the Israelites made their exit to hear God say, "If the people are faced with a battle, they might change their minds and return to Egypt" (Exod. 13:17 NLT). God had just miraculously rescued His beloved children from the yoke of slavery. They were walking out of the city with pockets full of jewels and precious metals and all the livestock they could herd. With such a display of power, provision, and authority, what could possibly cause the Israelites to change their minds? The answer: *unbelief.* They surveyed the long, dusty road ahead and allowed themselves to be overwhelmed by the impossibility of the situation rather than believing in the God of possibilities. Oh, how I can relate!

The opposite of doubt is faith. The writer of Hebrews defined it for us: "Now faith is confidence in what we hope for and assurance about what we do not see" (11:1). In the Greek, *confidence* is *hupostasis*, a combination of the Greek word *hypo*, meaning "under," and *histemi*, meaning "to stand." Figuratively, *confidence* means standing under a guaranteed agreement to have a legitimate claim.[9]

> **We have to believe the God of possibilities rather than be overwhelmed by the impossibility of our situation.**

We are children of the one true God, coheirs with Christ, and have a legitimate claim to an abundant future, even if we can't see it. With God, all things are possible! And we all say, "We believe! Doubt be gone. Faith be found."

ONLY GOD

My days of writing thank-you notes, coding bills, and caring for monthly givers ended almost twelve years after I accepted God's invitation to move. Yes, my *next thing* lasted twelve years. Sorry if that rains on your parade. Some seasons of waiting last longer than others.

My cubicle days were rich in character building. As I immersed myself in the study of God's Word, I fell more in love with God and less in love with me. Greater value was placed on bringing glory to His name rather than fame to mine. The truth of Philippians 2:3 took root deep in the once-rocky soil of my heart: "Do nothing out of selfish ambition or vain conceit. Rather, in humility value others above yourselves."

My *next thing* taught me that my purpose is not to stand at center stage, but to support the One who stands at center stage. His plan is always about His book, not mine. The picture finally became abundantly clear to me: it's only about God.

David knew everything revolved around God because He was all David had. David's family didn't pay much attention to him. They didn't even call him in from the field to be part of the sacrifice when Samuel came for a visit. For all David knew, his whole life was slated to be a shepherd, with God as his constant companion. Scripture gives no evidence that he dreamed of or had any other ambition. Yet God chose David as king and set him on a path to ready him for that responsibility. Once anointed, David simply did the next thing until he finally wore the king's crown. Until that day, he demonstrated confidence in God to complete the plan no matter who unexpectedly joined him on the journey.

What we learn in one wait prepares us for the next wait.

THIS PRINCIPLE IN THEIR PAUSE

Ashley moved forward and willingly served God wherever He called her to serve. First, she led a Bible study in her home to a small group of women from her Sunday school class. Second, she kept leading

worship for women's ministry events at her church. Later, she part-
nered to coteach a summer Bible study with another teacher who
already had an established Bible study group. During that time, she
accepted any invitation God placed in her path. She never stopped
moving. Often, she was asked to fill in teaching her Sunday morning
small group. Each opportunity grew her faith. Then came a joyful,
unexpected pause: motherhood. The momentum she had acquired
along the way had brought her to another call to wait and see.

Samantha recognized that her husband was not simply going
to knock on her door one day; she would have to take steps to meet
him. This meant leaving her comfort zone and trusting God. She
prayed for wisdom, and she agreed to say yes to whatever opportunities the Lord presented, which included filming a video with
Compassion International in El Salvador, signing up for online dating, becoming more active in church, and writing consistently on
her blog. As someone who tends to be introverted, Samantha found
these activities stretched her yet caused her to lean harder into God
and Proverbs 16:3: "Commit to the LORD whatever you do, and he
will establish your plans."

Dianna experienced a broken heart when her family lost their
home. They lost their happy place full of Christmas memories, first
steps, first bikes, and first days of school. One of their five moves took
her family into a place that felt nothing like home no matter how
hard she tried. Dianna wanted to move out the minute she moved
in. She secretly cried every time she walked in the door. But God
entwined Himself with her family, and memories became miracles.

Our story: Our biggest obstacle was fear. *What if Scott lost all
vision in the left eye? What if he lost his sight in both eyes?* Scott held

on to what he knew: God was still there. But the wait did not move Scott closer to God or to me. Most of the time, we felt as if we were facing the uncertainty alone, even isolated from each other. We *knew* God was there, but we didn't really talk about Him or our unanswered prayer.

THIS PRINCIPLE IN YOUR PAUSE

Now it's your turn. Use the "Worth the Wait" pages in chapter 10 to examine your current wait in light of the wait principles outlined in this chapter.

Here are some prompts to help you get started:

How do I respond when God asks me to move and/or change?

What is God asking me to change?

What is the greatest obstacle I face? Wavering? Fear? Confidence? Selfishness? Unbelief?

Am I obeying or delaying?

Digging Deeper with David: Psalm 56

Read Psalm 56.

God often requires us to change when we are waiting. It's not a popular idea because most of us don't like change. In this chapter, we learned the obstacles of moving. I want to take a longer look at fear, one of the biggest stumbling blocks to God's invitation to move.

David faced a variety of things most people would fear, such as wild animals, a giant Philistine, and unkind big brothers. We also find him face to face with another enemy, King Achish, leader of the Philistine army. It's important to note that David was not confronting the enemy on the battlefield. He and his army were hoping to "blend in" with the Philistine army in an effort to hide from King Saul, the lunatic.

David fled to the enemy territory of Gath. Isn't it ironic? David felt safer in enemy territory than in his homeland. Our giant-killing, victorious warrior, and soon-to-be king, was dealing with the very real emotion of fear.

WHEN I AM AFRAID

Read the first part of Psalm 56:3 aloud.

Using the blanks, respond by completing the sentence "When I am afraid …" Be honest. Don't give the Sunday school answer.

When I am afraid, _____

_____

What did David do when he was afraid?

_____

_____

It's only fair for me to share my answer since you were willing to share yours. When I am afraid, I tell someone and that someone usually isn't God. Then I try to resolve the issue myself. Eventually, after I have exhausted all my efforts, I finally turn to God.

David's example is the right one to follow. He told God, "I put my trust in you." Trust is hard when the enemy is nipping at your heels, the bills are unpaid, and your spouse decides to try life without you. David didn't wake up on this particular day and decide to put his trust in God. He didn't face King Achish and think, *This is a great time for me to trust God.*

Trusting God is a lifestyle. David knew it. David lived it. This lesson will help us learn and live the lifestyle of trusting God.

> *"Feed your faith, and your fears will starve*
> *to death." —Author unknown*

My first experience flying the friendly skies was at the tender age of thirty-five. This is my philosophy on air travel: if God meant for me to fly, He would have given me wings. The thought of flying then and now makes me shake in my shoes. My husband, however, feels quite comfortable up in the wild blue yonder, which is a good thing because his job requires significant air travel.

Until a few short years ago, my biggest fear was losing my husband in a plane crash. I feared being a young widow. Just typing these words makes me shudder. Fear consumed me each time I watched him walk through the airport door labeled "Departures." The fear depleted my energy and confidence. I had allowed my fears to starve me rather than permit my faith to sustain me.

God's truth is the nourishment for our faith. We feed our faith, and we starve our fears, with every truth we digest. The answer for my "young widow" fear will most likely apply to your greatest fear as well.

Read 2 Corinthians 10:5.

What does Paul tell us to do with every thought?

_____

Fear sets itself up against God's Word and pretends to be true. But our fears are demolished when we make them obey God's Word. This pretend truth did not remove my "young widow" fear. God's truth told me not to fear (Isa. 41:10). Moreover, it said God would not only strengthen me but also hold me up. So I fed my faith and made my fear bow to His truth.

> *"How very little can be done under the spirit*
> *of fear." —Florence Nightingale*

How true, Ms. Nightingale, how true! When our faith is starved, and our fear is nourished, our productivity becomes paralyzed. Yielding to a spirit of fear prevents us from accomplishing daily responsibilities and participating in kingdom change. A spirit of fear is not of God. Rather, it is a tool in the enemy's arsenal he uses to achieve his agenda for our life. Thankfully, our paralysis is reversed when we act on God's truth.

Write 2 Timothy 1:7 in the blanks below. Draw a line through what God does not give. Circle what He does give. (Keep in mind that *timid* means *fear*.)

_____

_____

_____

Notice that the list of what God gives is larger than the list of what He does not give. He always gives more than we can ever ask or imagine.

"Fear: False Evidence Appearing Real." —Author unknown

Though lots of false evidence surrounded David, he made the decision to trust in God. Our enemy will present false evidence to invoke fear, and that fear will cause us to doubt God's love and protection. Our enemy is the master of making evidence appear real. Just like a rearview mirror distorts the proximity of approaching cars, fear distorts what is true in an attempt to weaken our faith.

Even though false evidence may appear real and overwhelming, we don't have to allow it to overtake us. Our God—who we don't see—is greater than all we may perceive. With these truths in our arsenal, we can send fear packing!

5

When Waiting Messes with My Mind

Moving to my cute three-by-three-foot cubicle took me by surprise. While I loved my coworkers and my job, serving in the office rather than speaking on the stage created internal struggles. Doubt and lack of confidence taunted me. An old script haunted me: "You heard God wrong. You aren't qualified. Forget any notions you have about doing more." I came to realize that the longer my wait, the more I could expect such battles in my heart and mind.

Surely there had to be a way to combat these mounting fears—and somewhere I could turn for refuge when I was exhausted from the fight. As I faced my conflicts, I sought solace in my weekly Bible study. The teacher issued the class a challenge to enhance our prayer life: "We have to take our places on our faces."[10] Her suggestion really made me think. I was desperate for victory and a new nearness to God. Deep in my spirit, I knew I had to accept the challenge. I'd been praying fervently, but after hearing her words, I knew I had to take things up a notch … well, down a notch.

Though her words intrigued me, I didn't rush home and try this new posture of prayer. To be honest, I wasn't warming up to the thought of putting my face on the carpet. Her words, however, wouldn't leave me alone. "Places on our faces" replayed in my mind like a favorite '80s hit. Finally, one morning, in fear and trembling, I moved from the seat to the floor and prayed.

> ***A physical position of humility ushered me into a spiritual position of humility.***

This move helped me focus more on God and His peace as I read my Bible, prayed, and praised Him—on my face. Having a better grip on Scripture and opening my heart to God calmed my soul and strengthened my resolve. Being on my face wasn't necessary to be victorious over my internal struggles. It simply signified to the Lord my willingness to be humble, and it gave me another opportunity to experience God in a more intimate way. A physical position of humility ushered me into a spiritual position of humility. It equipped me to fight, as I learned how to use Scripture, prayer, and praise in defense against doubt and defeat.

God has an upside-down kingdom; His way *up* is actually *down*. God lifts us up into His peace, joy, and wisdom when we lower ourselves—when we become humble and subject ourselves to His will and His way (as we discussed in chapter 3). Part of doing this is battling our unbelief and doubt, as we say, "God, I don't understand why it is taking so long, but I will trust You. You can see what I cannot." A good verse to memorize in times of waiting is "'For my thoughts are not your thoughts, neither are your ways my ways,' declares the LORD" (Isa. 55:8). Our waiting is effective when done through God's perspective. In order to gain His viewpoint, though, we must use the tools He's given us.

It took me some time and much practice, but I eventually discovered God has given us an arsenal of weapons we can and should use as we wait. The three main ones are abiding in His truth, praying, and praising. He also offers us a place of rest in Himself.

> *Our waiting is effective when done through God's perspective.*

Waiting well isn't easy. We can be still to know God, do the next thing, obey His instructions, be secure in His holiness, and still combat doubt and fear. I realize this news doesn't make you want to shout, "Yes! I am *so* ready to wait on God." Yet this is an opportune time to do just that. We're safer drawing close to God in a battle than being far from Him. When our wait takes longer than we had hoped, it's often tempting to quit. Let's battle the fears and internal struggles with the weapons accessible to us and learn to humbly take refuge in the Lord.

WEAPONS OF WAR

David is a perfect example for us to follow. He served for many years as a part-time shepherd for his father and a part-time harpist for Saul, even after David was anointed king. Though David did not fight King Saul for his rightful throne, he did wage war against his own fears and doubt. Maybe you can relate to his struggles.

Just when we think we've got patience, determination, and courage figured out, our enemy named *I Told You So* taunts and teases. *Quit* mocks us. Beside him stands *Defeat*. David conquered all of these, and we can too. Let's learn how.

Weapon #1: Truth

Perhaps our most powerful weapon is truth. Though mighty, truth is useless unless wielded. *I Told You So* taunts us with lies: *God really doesn't have a plan for you. You aren't worthy of being a mother. You don't have what it takes to be a godly wife. You deserve this trouble because of your sin.* Lies can be slain only with truth. The only way to recognize lies is to know truth. The only way to know truth is to read truth. David constantly reminded himself of God's truth when he felt down and out, which increased the more his notoriety became a thorn in Saul's side.

David moved from the pasture to the palace, as well as to the battlefield. After many victories, Saul agreed to David marrying his daughter Michal. From the outside looking in, one would think this family had the makings of a Norman Rockwell painting. Yet turmoil, envy, and deadly plots consumed Saul and threatened David.

Saul's jealousy of David raged and overtook him. On more than one occasion, he attempted to take David's life by throwing a spear at the young man. Talk about family dysfunction. After escaping Saul's weapon several times, David decided to flee to the wilderness to save his life. While on the run, he penned Psalm 57.

Remember that David didn't have a Bible to read back then. He had the history of his ancestors, who had recorded and orally passed down God's faithfulness and character. Drawing on this, David battled the enemy of *I Told You So* with this truth: "I cry out to God Most High, to God who fulfills his purpose for me…. For your steadfast love is great to the heavens, your faithfulness to the clouds" (vv. 2, 10 ESV). Double-check these words: "*who fulfills his purpose for me.*" These are truths David clung to as he waited to go from anointed king to appointed king. He would have been able to use them as a weapon against his internal struggles only because he had spent time learning about God (the equivalent to our studying the Bible today).

Don't grow weary if you aren't a regular Bible reader—just be determined to become one. Until then, tuck away this verse, which has defended me against *I Told You So* for many years: "We demolish arguments and every pretension that sets itself up against the knowledge of God, and we take captive every thought to make it obedient to Christ" (2 Cor. 10:5).

The giant *I Told You So* pretends that everything he says is true. It confidently shouts falsehoods in our direction, getting louder until we cower under their weight. Anything that pretends to be true should be silenced by truth. Let's look at an example of this truth's application.

I Told You So **says:**   You deserve this because of your sin.

Truth says: God is faithful and just to forgive your sin (1 John 1:9). He began a good work in you and is faithful to complete it (Phil. 1:6).

When we apply biblical truth to lies, they die. The more truth we put in our minds, the greater power we have to defeat deceit. The more we know Scripture, the greater our arsenal against the enemy. It also gives us a right view on God's majesty; understanding His power and love is humbling and creates a longing to be holy as He is holy.

When we apply biblical truth to lies, they die.

A simple word search of Scripture—either online or in the back of a Bible—will bring up verses we can use as weapons. You may want to write down these verses on a notecard to keep on your bathroom mirror, in your purse, next to your bed, or on your desk. Or try writing your own psalm, as David did. Recall God's goodness, faithfulness, and power. Also, many musicians have turned Scripture into songs. Listen to those as a way to memorize Scripture so it is a weapon at the ready when you need to battle insecurity.

Weapon #2: Prayer

Prayer slays the giant *Quit.* One wait after another … followed by the next thing … sprinkled with an *I Told You So*—all of this will make a girl want to give up. Long waits cause us to say, "Forget it, Lord. This is too hard. I'm finished. I'm out." We have to double down and put behind prayer all the training we've learned in our wait. Then we wield it. Quitting is not an option.

As I waited to become pregnant, several situations piled on top of one another that required my action. Decisions needed to be made; deadlines had to be met. If they weren't, my wait would be even longer. That thought loomed over me as I repeated pros and cons of every possibility of every decision. All this made me bone weary. The injections, charts, doctor appointments—it all became too much. I found myself on the edge of giving up trying to conceive.

In exhaustion, I paused from the frenzy, bowed my head, and humbly sought the Lord for His ways. "Lord, what am I supposed to do? How is this going to work? Help me replace the object of my wait with You, the God of my faith." Peace filled me as *Quit* lost its power.

Similarly, David came to a point where he stood on the brink of giving up being king. In 1 Samuel 27, David was on the run—again—from the ruthless Saul. Tired of fighting to stay alive, "David kept thinking to himself, 'Someday Saul is going to get me. The best thing I can do is escape to the Philistines. Then Saul will stop hunting for me in Israelite territory, and I will finally be safe'" (v. 1 NLT). He was just over it. Done.

Have you ever wanted to head for the hills and wipe your hands of it all? The first few years after Kelly had said, "I do," she wanted to yell, "I don't anymore!" Little annoyances blew up into massive fights. She and her husband argued over whose utensils they would use, which direction to mow the yard, and how often to balance their checkbook. Kelly figured the tension would ease after a while, but the longer she waited, the harder things seemed to be. She eventually reached a near-breaking point and contemplated divorce. Kelly didn't believe things could ever be peaceful between her and Jake. Thankfully, they spent time in a counselor's office, in prayer, and in the Word, learning what it meant to be a godly husband and wife. This eased Kelly away from the edge of ending her marriage; now, ten years later, they are still together.

Kelly needed hope that things could change, that she and Jake wouldn't argue over every little thing. Because her marriage was in disrepair for so long, she did not believe it would ever be fixed. We all struggle with unbelief at times when we feel on the brink of quitting, don't we? I like what Matthew Henry's commentary says about David's despair: "Unbelief is a sin that easily besets even good men, when without are fightings, and within are fears; and it is a hard matter to get over them."[11] At the root of wanting to quit is unbelief, which we must battle. One of the best ways to do so is meeting with the Lord in prayer.

You might be thinking, *All this sounds good, but I don't know how to pray. And do I have to lie on the carpet?* I understand those thoughts. For years, it seemed my prayers bounced off the ceiling. I thought there was a special formula to prayer and someone had forgotten to give it to me. Then I discovered the big secret: The key to a successful prayer life is to pray. We don't have to be a Bible scholar or have vast knowledge of Scripture. Prayer is a simple conversation with God birthed out of a humble heart to simply seek Him.

The key to a successful prayer life is to pray.

Jesus taught us how to pray and instructed us not to use big, lofty, meaningless words. His model for prayer is simple: "Our Father in heaven, may your name always be kept holy. May your kingdom come and what you want be done, here on earth as it is in heaven. Give us the food we need for each day. Forgive us for our sins, just as we have forgiven those who sinned against us. And do not cause us to be tempted, but save us from the Evil One" (Matt. 6:9–13 NCV).

The power isn't in the words you say or if you're standing, sitting, or even swimming! The power is in the One we pray to—God. Lying on my face is something God led me to do to humble myself during a desperate season. You may not need a lesson in humility like yours truly. But if you do, remember that humility is demonstrated by your heart's submission, not your physical position.

The giant *Quit* is not easily defeated, so prayer must be repeated. James 5:16 tells of the power we have when we pray: "The prayer of a righteous person is powerful and effective." And Paul instructs us to "never stop praying" (1 Thess. 5:17 NLT). If you are looking for a prayer reference book to get started, try praying some of David's heartfelt words in his psalms. The more we pray, the stronger we become and the more able we are to take down *Quit*.

Weapon #3: Praise

Praise has a marvelously mysterious aspect to it that slays *Defeat*. Singing praises can lift the head of a destitute man, comfort a heart-broken widow, encourage a wayward teenager, and defeat an enemy.

As David waited, his opponent repeatedly tried to deter him from becoming king. It must have been humbling for this mighty man of war and valor to be so powerless. One day, King Saul sent men to David's home to seize and kill him. David made his escape by climbing out a window and running away. Talk about feeling defeated! Even so, in this bleak portion of his wait, he renewed his trust in God's plans for him. His faith is seen in these words of praise: "But I will sing of your strength; I will sing aloud of your steadfast love in the morning. For you have been to me a fortress and a refuge in the day of my distress. O my Strength, I will sing praises to you, for you, O God, are my fortress, the God who shows me steadfast love" (Ps. 59:16–17 ESV).

Let's look at another story from the Old Testament to show the power of praise. Three armies surrounded the southern kingdom of Israel and threatened to annihilate them. Israel's king, Jehoshaphat, prayed to the Lord for guidance. God answered him by saying he should lead Israel's army to face the three other armies, with the promise that God Himself would defeat them. As you can imagine, this overjoyed Jehoshaphat.

Before he led his army to the battle, he sent the choir and the men of Israel to the front lines with instructions to praise God. "After consulting the people, Jehoshaphat appointed men to sing to the LORD and to praise him for the splendor of his holiness as they went out at the head of the army, saying: 'Give thanks to the LORD, for his love endures forever'" (2 Chron. 20:21).

I am not a general and know very little about war, but sending a choir ahead to sing praises would not be part of my battle strategy. Even though it sounds like a crazy military operation, Jehoshaphat followed the instructions based on his confidence in God's promise of victory. The choir's joyous singing confused the armies of Moab, Mt. Seir, and Ammon. Being caught off guard by the concert, they weren't able to contend against the Lord's ambush. The predicted victor succumbed to defeat as Israel, the underdog, worshipped God.

In the wait, praise doesn't seem like an obvious tactic for victory. Might I add, it's difficult to muster the energy or enthusiasm to sing in the face of defeat and discouragement. In such circumstances, praise takes effort and often feels insincere. I can testify from personal experience, though, that the energy it takes to praise is replenished by the uplifting your soul receives. Our actual enemies may not fall as the armies of Moab, Mt. Seir, and Ammon did, but the spirit of *Defeat* will not have victory over our mind, body, soul, or spirit.

THE UNEXPECTED HIDING PLACE

Reading the Bible, praying, and praising the Lord are wonderful weapons we should wield so often that they become as natural as breathing. They turn us toward God so that we find our rest and solace in Him rather than in things of this world. God wants to be our first refuge, yet it takes effort on our part to make Him just that.

I know getting lost in distractions is easier than taking time to know the Lord. Yet the only permanent and satisfying hiding place we'll ever have is God. It takes time and discipline to train ourselves to turn to Him first for rest. So what do we do in the interim before that becomes second nature? And how do we let go of the other things we've used to help us hide from *I Told You So*, *Quit*, and *Defeat*?

Wrong Places of Refuge

For years, I sought refuge in all the wrong places. Comfort came in an icy Dr Pepper and a pepperoni, ham, and pineapple thin-crust pizza. I'd follow that lunch up with a shopping spree, racking up loads of credit-card debt. Doing so helped me momentarily forget the difficulties of my wait. The thrill of finding a deal on clothes shielded me from the nagging negative whispers to my spirit.

What do you take refuge in—food, alcohol, gossip, excessive sleep, television, social media? These promise to take us away from the pain and frustration, and they usually do, for a few minutes.

Rather than reading our Bible for encouragement, we click on the trending celebrity news. Instead of talking to God, we text our friends. I will be the first to admit I can spend hours connecting the dots on the app Free Flow or binge watching my favorite television shows. Where do you turn for comfort when doubt and insecurity rage against you? Hopefully, it's not in a wild place like the Philistine camp that David sought out!

David defeated his internal struggles through truth, prayer, and praise many times over. But when he was on the run from Saul, he didn't always think clearly. Despite years of experience surviving in the pasture, David sought refuge in the Philistine camp—the very army he had been fighting! But when the Philistines rejected him, David escaped to the land of Adullam and found refuge in a cave— yes, a cave (1 Sam. 22:1).

The Right Place of Refuge

God is purposeful with every word He inspired to be written in the Bible. You are going to love this, even if you aren't a word nerd. The word *Adullam* means "refuge." Are you as wowed by that as I am? Our right place of refuge and vindication is God. He reminded David of this by bringing the anointed king to a figurative and literal haven. God knew David's circumstances, as well as his state of mind. He thought it best for David to be far from the distractions and worries around him, which would give him time to reflect on truth, to pray, and to praise.

Sometimes I need to get away from the everyday commotion around me to rest in God. Personally, that means waking up an hour before my family so I have time alone with the Lord. In those quiet moments, I am better able to focus on God. It seems that applied to David as well. While in the cave of Adullam, David penned Psalm 57. Let's ingest some of his words:

> Have mercy on me, my God, have mercy on me,
> for in you I take refuge.
> I will take refuge in the shadow of your wings
> until the disaster has passed.
>
> I cry out to God Most High,
> to God, who vindicates me.
> He sends from heaven and saves me,
> rebuking those who hotly pursue me—
> God sends forth his love and his faithfulness.
> (vv. 1–3)

David recognized his place of protection and restoration was found in God. Perhaps my favorite part of this passage is "I will take refuge in the shadow of your wings until the disaster has passed." David's words speak to impatient hearts to simply wait it out and rest in God's refuge.

As David sat in the cave of Adullam—the place of refuge—he also wrote Psalm 34. I find it interesting that not once did he ask God any who, what, when, where, why, or how questions. Instead, he humbly recalled truth, prayed, and praised the Lord. "This poor man called, and the LORD heard him; he saved him out of all his troubles" (v. 6).

The word *poor* in the Hebrew is *'ā-nî*, which means "humble." This mighty warrior—slayer of bears, fighter of lions, killer of giants—had come to rely on God's abilities rather than his own. Instead of demanding to know God's timeline, he rested in God's trustworthiness. Rather than taking on King Saul and his armies, he took a backseat to God's greater plans.

However and wherever we escape to reset ourselves physically, spiritually, or mentally, we should make sure to go to the right place of refuge: God. In fact, we have a standing invitation to do just that. As Jesus traveled and spoke in Galilee, He implored the crowds:

> Come to me, all you who are weary and burdened, and I will give you rest. Take my yoke upon you and learn from me, for I am gentle and humble in heart, and you will find rest for your souls. For my yoke is easy and my burden is light. (Matt. 11:28–30)

Maybe you are like me and revel in the thought of exchanging your weariness for rest. You are tired of fighting and working hard all the time. You've said and done all the "right" things, only to end up hiding alone in a cave. Let the words of Jesus calm your anxiousness. Try reading them once more, this time in a different translation:

> Are you tired? Worn out? Burned out on religion? Come to me. Get away with me and you'll recover your life. I'll show you how to take a real rest. Walk with me and work with me—watch how I do it. Learn the unforced rhythms of grace. I won't lay

anything heavy or ill-fitting on you. Keep company
with me and you'll learn to live freely and lightly.
(THE MESSAGE)

TRAINING TIME

Have you ever wondered how much David practiced using a sling-
shot while he tended his sheep? While the duties of a shepherd
are time consuming, he had hours to allow the sheep to graze and
finesse his skills. Lions and bears roamed the hills he tended, so we
can be sure he had ample opportunity to take down many animals
to protect his herd. That prepared him to be an outstanding soldier
and king.

Waiting on God isn't wasting time; it's training time. Whether
we are humbly tending to "sheep" in our pasture, moving to our
next thing, standing on the battlefield, or hiding in a cave, we must
practice using our weapons—spending time in the Word, praying,
and praising. Doing so will take down *I Told You So*, *Quit*, and
Defeat. Then, we must take time to know God as we hide out in
Him. Keeping company with God is how we learn to wait well, fight
our inner battles, and find rest.

THIS PRINCIPLE IN THEIR PAUSE

Ashley received an unexpected call from her adoption agency.
Even though she and her husband were convinced placement was
at least another year away, God had different plans. The minute her
baby boy was placed into her arms, she knew life would change.

And change it did! She left her career and settled into her new role as mom. She set aside her heart's desire to speak, teach, and write Bible studies. She believed God, but at times she struggled with feelings of doubt when she would see other moms who were writing and speaking. Caught between real life and her dream, she remembered the lesson she had learned before—stay willing, stay humble, and keep her eyes on Him. She journeyed on, knowing it was better to trust in God than trust in her feelings.

Samantha had been waiting fifteen years to be married. Though she was loving God and others, learning to trust in God's timing and will, and taking steps of obedience, she experienced times of sadness too. When discouragement set in, Samantha often turned to half-hour comedies on television and comfort food (especially mac 'n' cheese). Tuning out real life by tuning in to fictional characters offered a distraction from her wait. But while her spirits went up, so did her pants size. Samantha came to realize that the sad times didn't last forever, and she found a better way to handle them. One strategy included focusing on the comfort in Psalm 30:5: "Weeping may last through the night, but joy comes with the morning" (NLT).

Dianna took a low-paying, hourly job until God healed her mind, heart, and body from years of stress during the wait. The job was an hour from home, but she needed to be with the people who worked there just as much as she needed the money. Days turned into years, but her healing came through His love and by the hands of the precious people she worked with. She faithfully wielded her weapons of truth, prayer, and praise, never allowing *I Told You So*, *Quit*, or *Defeat* to have victory. One tiny step at a time, she and her family pressed through what seemed would never end into a good place.

Our story: While I wielded all three weapons, Scott fought with prayer and truth. He refused to submit to *Defeat*. As he listened to the whispers of the Holy Spirit and leaned into what He knew (the nearness of God), Scott made the decision to move from his local doctors to a specialist at a nationally recognized clinic in another state. But the side effects from all the meds began to take their toll on Scott, which in turn took their toll on our marriage. Silence ruled, and survival became our theme.

THIS PRINCIPLE IN YOUR PAUSE

Now it's your turn. Use the "Worth the Wait" pages in chapter 10 to examine your current wait in light of the lessons outlined in this chapter.

Here are some prompts to help you get started:

Identify your wrong places of refuge, and determine to walk away from them.

How can you use the weapons of truth, prayer, and praise more successfully in your life?

Digging Deeper with David: Psalm 37

Read Psalm 37.

Young David moved unexpectedly from the pasture to the battlefield (1 Sam. 17). His confidence to take on a giant is inspiring to this not-so-young woman. It's obvious at this point he was not experiencing any internal struggles.

Scripture did not record a conversation between God and David concerning Goliath. We never read, "God, do You want me to take care of this giant who keeps harassing Your people?" We witness externally David's internal relationship with God. He was so well acquainted with God that when the time came to act, he did.

This is the kind of relationship I want to have with God. This is the kind of relationship I want for you to have with God. By examining and applying David's relationship-building secrets, I am confident we can slay any giant we face.

RELATIONSHIP-BUILDING SECRETS

David's secrets have the potential to radically revolutionize our relationship with the Lord. In fact, I feel quite certain the effect of these secrets will spill out of us and onto others, improving all of our relationships. When our vertical relationship is strong, we are less likely to come unglued when experiencing trials and troubles in our horizontal relationships. What David teaches goes beyond pleasing God; he says we can *delight* God. Can you just imagine?

Secret #1: Don't Fret

David's first secret is a warning. This warning is so important that he repeated "don't fret" twice in eight verses.

The first secret is a threat to all the other secrets. *Fret* is the Hebrew word *charah*. David warns us not to be burned with anger, worry, and jealousy when evil seems to be overcoming good. We should be concerned with such behaviors but not consumed to the point we become distracted from pleasing God.

Our response to the evil and wrongdoing around us is found in Micah 6:8. Write out God's instructions for us in the space below.

_____

_____

Fretting is a "delight bandit." Just when we are enjoying a little happiness, it sneaks up and pickpockets our delight. David warned about its hazards after the second "do not fret" warning.

Read Psalm 37:8.

What happens when we continue to burn with anger, worry, and jealousy?

_____

Fretting replaces the peace that accompanies our delighting in God, thus keeping God from delighting in us. Fretting makes the wait longer. David suggests if we don't control fretting, it is possible to behave like the very people we are fretting over.

Read Philippians 4:6–7.

How does God want us to handle our anxious thoughts?

_____

What is the result of obeying verse 6?

_____

Secret #2: Trust

Trust *of* God grows through experience *with* God. Through our experiences of trusting God, life becomes lighter and almost tender at times. Troubles don't disappear, but the new measure of faith diminishes their intensity. A bonus of trusting God is delight: our delight in Him and His delight in us. We begin to long for what He longs for and love what He loves. Sounds like the kind of life that would make waiting a little easier.

Read Proverbs 3:5.

How do we demonstrate our trust in God?

_____

_____

Secret #3: Commit

Committing our ways to the Lord builds our trust. Our ways are difficult to surrender because we make decisions and plans based on what we see. God's plans are based on what He sees. We have to remember that His view extends beyond what we see and His knowledge exceeds what we know. Therefore, He proves Himself trustworthy of our ways.

What ways can you commit to the Lord?

_____

_____

Secret #4: Be Still

Does it seem your day passes by so fast that you are certain you pass yourself? Girls, we can't wait until we are not busy to be still and get to know God. We will never *not* be busy. We need to discipline ourselves to be still in the moment—that moment when we sense His presence or feel His Spirit. Just stop and be still.

Are you afraid of being still? If so, why? Be still and share your fears with God. Write a prayer expressing your thoughts and concerns.

_____

_____

6

When Waiting Meets the Unexpected

When God changes our environment, we may meet people we never anticipated being part of our story. He can use our pastor, our counselor, our boss, or a family member to teach and challenge us during our wait. God also uses people we wouldn't expect—people like my friend Sherri.

Sherri was an unexpected friend God invited to my wait. Even to this day, it's hard to believe we became such close friends. We are more different than alike. Sherri is soft spoken, and I am, well, not. Her color pallet is limited. Mine? Loud. Our family dynamics are also dissimilar, yet God connected our hearts through a common interest—music. Our love for worship bonded our hearts and grew a deep, godly friendship, completely unexpected by us both. She became a trusted confidant and reliable shoulder. God used this unexpected friendship to further teach me the beautiful freedom associated with being set apart.

It pains me to confess this to you: I was a CBS soap-opera-aholic. My afternoon lineup started with *The Young and the Restless* and ended with *Guiding Light*. It may seem silly to you that I could be addicted to daytime dramas, but these characters were like family. I was envious of their lives and what happened to them, and they were a regular part of my conversations with other people who also watched. As I drew near to God through obedience and the study of His Word, the behavior of the characters and story lines on their shows began to unsettle my spirit. However, I felt powerless to *not* turn on the television each afternoon. Sherri helped me gain the strength to overpower the pull of the remote control.

She did more than pray. On a regular basis, I would have an accountability voice-mail message from her that went something like this:

"Wendy? [Pause] It's Sherri. [Another very long pause.] It's three o'clock. [Pause] I was wondering what you are watching."

Who could turn the television on knowing a call like that could come at any time? She held me accountable to stand strong and wait well as God did His perfect work in my life to prepare me for the perfect timing of His plan.

Over the years, Sherri and I spent time unpacking scriptures in Bible study. We've served side by side in church ministry. We've even shared a tissue or two. Oh, the joys of this godly friendship I would have missed had I closed the door on the unexpected. Not only that, but my wait would have been miserable all alone.

I love the truth of Ecclesiastes 4:9: "Two people are better off than one, for they can help each other succeed" (NLT). David's son, King Solomon, penned these words. I can't help but wonder if he learned this lesson in part from his father. Indeed, two are better than one!

DAVID AND THE UNEXPECTED

When God placed unexpected people in David's life, he welcomed them. He accepted their help and wise counsel. His journey from the pasture to the palace was enriched when God surrounded him with three people who stood with him. Let's get acquainted with these key individuals.

Meet Jonathan: Son of David's Enemy
Value: Defended David's Character

The one who had the most to fear from David's military success and public hurrahs was the crown prince, Jonathan. That's right, the person in line for the throne—King Saul's son. He's the last person you would expect to become David's best friend and most loyal supporter. As one commentary puts it, "Two men, each on track for the same throne, yet they made a covenant of friendship that would prove stronger than jealousy, than envy, than ambition."[12] Instead of being consumed with resentment or trying to discredit David, Jonathan vowed to support David, even if it went against his father.

The friendship between David and Jonathan began after the meeting Saul had with David, following the defeat of Goliath. When the debriefing ended, David and Jonathan spoke privately. Scripture doesn't tell us what the two discussed, but we know how the conversation ended: "Jonathan took off the robe he was wearing and gave it to David, along with his tunic, and even his sword, his bow and his belt" (1 Sam. 18:4). Since most of us aren't heirs to a throne or robe-wearing royalty, let's unpack Jonathan's words so we can understand his actions:

His robe: He was the next likely candidate for the throne. By giving his robe, Jonathan conveyed to David, "I give you my rank, fame, and position."

His tunic: Jonathan's garments were symbolic of his military accomplishments. A soldier takes great pride in his uniform and honors. Jonathan was telling David, "Your merit and military success is more important than all I have or will ever achieve."

His sword: This was an incredible gift. At the time, Saul and Jonathan were the only people in Israel who owned swords. The Philistines prohibited the Israelites to make spears and swords. Jonathan gave David his most prized possession.

Jonathan's actions symbolized his acceptance that David would one day sit on the throne. Not only that, but this gesture showed that Jonathan truly believed David would be king—Jonathan was in it for the long haul and had committed to wait it out with David. To help David as he waited to be crowned king, Jonathan pledged his loyalty to his friend, even if that meant defying Saul (1 Sam. 19). Standing against his father and standing up for David became as natural as breathing for Jonathan; on more than one occasion, he defended David's character to Saul. He even thwarted Saul's plan to kill David (1 Sam. 20).

What was the source of this bond? How can two people so different be committed to such friendship and loyalty? The bond is God. He loved David and Jonathan so much that He gave them a beautiful friendship. God is the greatest knitter of hearts. When another's heart is committed to ours, that person will stand with us in our wait and help ward off the naysayers.

Perhaps each of us is someone's unexpected friend waiting to be found. What if we reached out to other women? Maybe start a neighborhood pray-as-you-walk group or game-and-dessert night. As we get to know these women, a friendship will form and hearts will be knit together. As we listen, we'll learn about their waits and how we can stand with them. We can always expect the unexpected from God, even when it comes to unique friends.

A friend defends and builds godly character.

Meet Michal: Daughter of David's Enemy
Value: Displayed Love

Saul's jealousy of David consumed him. He moved David from musician in the palace to head of the armies on the battlefield. The king didn't intend this promotion to be a blessing, but rather to put David in harm's way. And it was another move David accepted without complaint. Just as he had done as a shepherd and musician, he served well as a soldier and leader, and God blessed him.

Saul's attempt to end David's life failed, and David became more successful and even more popular among the people. In fact, a prevalent chant among the Israelites was "Saul has slain his thousands and David his tens of thousands." As you can imagine, Saul grew angrier and even more determined to end David's life.

In the midst of the warring, love unexpectedly bloomed. Saul's daughter Michal (me-kawl) fell in love with David. Talk about salt in the wound! First, Saul's son befriended David; now his daughter wanted to be betrothed to him. Yet Saul viewed the pending marriage as a way to entrap David. He agreed to give his daughter to David in marriage with one stipulation. Saul demanded an unusual dowry, which he hoped would get David killed as he procured it. "Tell David that all I want for the bride price is 100 Philistine foreskins!

Vengeance on my enemies is all I really want" (1 Sam. 18:25 NLT). However, much to Saul's chagrin, David paid the dowry and married Michal.

While David was on harp duty one evening, Saul's tormented spirit overwhelmed the king. On impulse, Saul made an attempt on David's life. As Saul's spear flew toward David, he escaped and fled to Michal. The king sent his men to Michal's house to watch for David to kill him, but they didn't get the chance. "But Michal, David's wife, warned him, 'If you don't run for your life tonight, tomorrow you'll be killed.' So Michal let David down through a window, and he fled and escaped" (1 Sam. 19:11–12).

You and I will probably never need to escape a maniacal king or climb out a window to spare our own lives. But we may one day need a friend to come to our aid during our wait. As David waited to be king, he continued to do what he knew—serve as a musician and soldier for King Saul. Michal displayed her love for her husband by risking her own life to help him escape. She put her own needs aside so David could be safe.

You and I can show the same love to others needing a helping hand as they wait. This might mean getting up early to meet for coffee so you can listen to your friend. Simply talking about the fear and doubt helps others break away from them. Maybe you take your friend out for dinner on girls' night. A fun evening of laughter is a sweet release from the angst of waiting. Sharing tears always relieves the weariness and loneliness of the wait too. Whether we are on the receiving end or giving end of sacrificial love, let's be bold and courageous, as Michal was.

A friend loves and makes sacrifices.

Meet Samuel: Israel's Priest
Value: Distracted the Enemy at Ramah

It's to be expected that David had a priest in his life, but what that priest did for David was quite unexpected. Samuel and David no doubt had a special bond because Samuel had the privilege of anointing David as the future king. Samuel became a close confidant to David. In one particular instance, he also served as David's distraction from his enemy.

David was on the run again. (Willie Nelson's hit "On the Road Again" is playing in my mind.) After his near-death experience climbing out of Michal's window, David escaped to Ramah to seek refuge and counsel from Samuel. He lamented and poured his heart out to this godly friend, and perhaps he asked Samuel some hard questions, such as, "Why is this happening to me? God anointed me king! I have obeyed Him. When He told me to leave the pasture, I did. When He instructed me to play the harp for Saul, I did. Did I misunderstand Him? Did I hear Him wrong?" We have asked similar questions when our waiting has become difficult.

> **We need individuals who will stand with
> us while we're under attack.**

Samuel took David to his home in Naioth to hide him as he waited for Saul to end his manhunt. This distraction threw Saul and his men off David's scent, at least for a while. The Naioth hideaway provided David a place to rest and refuel while his weak faith strengthened.

Our enemy never gives up on his pursuit of our destruction. He is ruthless. We need individuals who will shelter us when we are under attack. This could be a family member who commits to pray for us, or a friend who texts us a Bible verse every day, or a close confidant who regularly does a heart check by asking, "Are you feeling weary? Has your faith waned? What can I do to encourage you?" Samuel willingly provided a place of refuge and rest for David; let's accept the same help from our family and friends and be sure to offer it to others.

In the perils of our wait, it's a wonderful blessing to have a band of friends, even two or three, who will join us on the front lines of battle. Samuel isn't the only example of such a companion in the Bible. Shadrach, Meshach, and Abednego stood together on the front lines of an actual fire. Eliphaz, Bildad, and Zophar sat with Job in his misery for seven days and never uttered a word.

Who springs to your mind as a faithful friend in tough times? Maybe someone who has brought you dinner, watched your kids, sent you a Bible verse, or simply listened to your heart. One of my favorite trios in Scripture is Moses and his friends Aaron and Hur. Their loving example hits close to home for me. "When Moses' hands grew tired, they took a stone and put it under him and he sat on it. Aaron and Hur held his hands up—one on one side, one on the other—so that his hands remained steady till sunset" (Exod. 17:12).

Moses sent Joshua into battle to fight. While Joshua and the men waged war, Moses stood on top of the mountain, holding his staff over the valley. As long as Moses held up the staff, Joshua and his men experienced victory; however, when he lowered the staff, their enemies gained momentum.

Moses's friends followed him up the mountain. Aaron and Hur could see the pressure and agony Moses faced. To ease Moses's suffering, these friends each supported one of his arms as he held the staff high. They couldn't hold the staff *for* Moses, but they could stand *with* him through the long battle. They filled the gap created by Moses's weakness with their strength.

Aaron and Hur moved from being bystanders to being gap standers. A bystander is an onlooker who watches but does not get involved. A gap stander has empathy and takes action, using their strength to help the fighter stand until victory comes. A gap stander provides a safe place for the one in battle to rest.

A few years ago, several friends took on the role of gap standers for me. They held me up and strengthened my weak faith as I watched my daughter battle an enemy only she could fight.

Middle school is a stinky time, for parents and for teens. These young people don't know which end is up or what direction to take. Parents do a lot of praying and pacing.

From the time she was eighteen months old, Blaire frequently had a book in her hand. She would even read at night under the covers with a book light. Her books had become her friends, and she spent hours upon hours nurturing her relationships. The middle school years hit my daughter hard. As they progressed, Blaire lifted her nose above the top of her book and realized she'd better make some friends outside of the pages. One problem, though: by this time, friend groups had already formed.

This momma's heart suffered as I achingly watched her withdraw into a small world of one. Little by little, the sparkle of her green eyes dimmed. Her beautiful smile rarely made an appearance. The laughter that once bellowed from her belly was seldom heard.

As much as I wanted to help Blaire establish meaningful relationships and slay the giant of depression, it was a fight she had to win alone. Her father and I, as well as other godly people, had introduced her to faith in Jesus, but now she had to discover for herself what a life built on her own faith meant. While I gripped Blaire's arms and pushed a rock under her, my friends held my arms and gave me a rock on which to rest.

On the sidelines of her struggle, as I waved the banner of my faith and prayed for Blaire, my gap standers lifted me up in prayer. The Holy Spirit led me to verses to help strengthen Blaire's resolve. My friends sent spiritual nourishment to sustain me. It seemed just when I needed encouragement, one of my warriors would call just to say, "How are you?" These dear women stood with me so I could stand with my daughter.

As a result of this great battle, Blaire is a young woman of faith, strong and wise beyond her years. Her convictions are rock solid, and her life is governed by God's Word and His Spirit in her. I'm convinced this is true because of the trials she endured. The battles we face in our wait prepare us for the next place in our adventure with God. He stands with us and gives friends a front-row seat to witness His display of glory.

A friend distracts the enemy and stands in the gap to strengthen us when the wait weakens our faith.

WHAT IF I DON'T HAVE ONE OF THOSE?

The most valuable unexpected friends I have in my seasons of wait are God, His Spirit, and His Word. They defend my character, display love, and distract my enemies. The emergence of their friendship has been years in the making.

In my pastor's study, at the tender age of seven, I surrendered my heart to Jesus. My parents gave me the *Children's Living Bible* with a watercolor picture of Jesus on the cover to commemorate my life-changing decision.

When I first became a Christian, I didn't know God, the Holy Spirit, and the Bible could be my friends. That's why I hail them as the greatest unexpected confidants I've had as I've waited. These three are always with me and for me. Their counsel is spot-on and unbiased. Their instructions always take me where I am supposed to be—maybe not where I want to be, but where I am supposed to be.

> ### *I did not know God, the Holy Spirit, and the Bible could be my friends.*

It may sound odd or impossible to have God or a book as a friend. You may be thinking, *I don't have even one godly friend I can invite to coffee. How do I get God to be my friend?*

As in any other relationship, time cultivates growth. The more you spend time with God through prayer and in His Word, the deeper your love for Him will grow. Before you know it, you will call Him friend too. While it's a beautiful life to have and cultivate a friendship with God, let's be real: sometimes we need a friend with skin.

God created us for human companionship. In fact, it's one of the reasons He made Eve for Adam—we are meant to have relationships with other people. While this sounds good, as an adult, it can be hard to find and cultivate friendships. The older I get, the more I recognize this.

We get busy with our family, work, home, and hobbies. Before we know it, our friends fade into mere acquaintances, and the only way we keep up with them is by "liking" their photographs on Instagram or Facebook. Time is a valuable commodity, and we often worry about being a burden to a friend's calendar when we ask her for support during our wait. Therefore, we can quickly find ourselves feeling lonely if we are not proactive in cultivating connections.

Starting and maintaining a relationship with anyone, be it our spouse, our sister, or a girlfriend, takes time and effort. In elementary school, it seemed as easy as sharing our dolls or pushing each other on the swings. Now we have to give more to build a community around us and let go of some of our concerns of being a burden.

I have always struggled with the confidence to reach out and meet new people. Wherever you fall on the shy-versus-bold scale, here are some basic strategies to make friends:

A good place to start is by joining a small group at church, going to a mommy's morning-out group, or volunteering. You'll find like-minded people who are probably in a similar season of life as you are. Call your church office or local nonprofit to see what openings are available.

Get to know your neighbors. Long gone are the days when people spent evenings on their front porches or met with their neighbors for a block party. You could be the one to revive that! My husband and I began to meet our neighbors on our morning walks. Because Scott has stopped to talk with people as he drives in from work, he has found friends to share tools and equipment. Take every opportunity to stop and chat.

Once you've established a friendship, remember these more specific strategies:

Discern if that person provides a safe place to share your heart. Look for a friend who is trustworthy, forgives, and lifts others up. Find someone who offers to pray and points you to the Word and God. Ideally, we want to weave our friendship with God, the Holy Spirit, and the Bible into our friendships with people.

Determine if the individual is in a season of life to support you in your wait. Some people might not be, and that's okay. If they are, that's great.

Discuss your situation and share your story. Ask her if she would be willing to pray for you, check in on you every now and then, and encourage you with truth along the way. Then ask how you can be a good friend to her. Make a commitment to be available, and follow up on that with a regular text message, coffee date, or phone call.

Risk is involved any time we reach out to others and open our heart. But there are also great rewards: support, hope, and encouragement. First, take the time to develop a strong friendship with God, the Holy Spirit, and the Bible through prayer and reading. They are the best front line to defend our character, display love, and distract the enemy. Next, find and nurture relationships with others who will support you, and whom you can support.

THIS PRINCIPLE IN THEIR PAUSE

Ashley reluctantly accepted wisdom and encouragement from her husband during the early season of motherhood. God always used him to speak truth into her reality when she was more apt to live by feelings. Her primary responsibilities at home were far more important than speaking, teaching, and writing. At first, she didn't accept the truth of his words because they hurt. It felt as though someone were stepping on her calling. As she prayed through her feelings, the Lord calmed her heart, reminded her of the value of her present calling, and reconfirmed that He had not forgotten His call on her life. During this interval, God opened a few opportunities to speak at women's events outside her church and brought a writing mentor into her life. Being able to hear encouragement from women through another season of waiting allowed her to grow deep roots of faith and not give up.

Samantha received encouragement from family and friends in their own ways. One family member gave her cooking lessons. A group of girlfriends initiated an annual out-of-town spiritual retreat. Another friend served others alongside Samantha. From a simple text message with a Bible verse, to a walk through downtown, to gardening together, the Lord used different people at different times to remind Samantha of His goodness. One thing each person had in common was that she continually pointed Samantha to the grander plan the Lord has for His children—to glorify God and enjoy Him for eternity. This helped Samantha stay focused on the Person of her faith more than the object of her wait. Through every peak and valley, her family and friends lived out Proverbs 17:17, "A friend loves at all times."

Dianna witnessed God use unexpected people to keep her family going over the years of wait. He was visibly faithful every single day. Like the time someone she didn't even know sold them a car for her son for one dollar. Her brother sold her a fifteen-thousand-dollar car for three hundred dollars. A friend paid the first month's rent while others gave a washing machine and dryer. She will never forget the contributions of others in providing a paid vacation, health insurance that saved her life, a $10,000 check, and a computer for her to be able to work and write—and the most surprising, a dream job for her husband.

Our story: An unexpected friend came back in Scott's life. Jerry's enthusiasm and joy in the Lord was a welcome distraction to Scott. Jerry faithfully prayed for Scott, even anointing him with oil. At one point, Jerry pulled him from the office and into a fishing boat to help take Scott's mind off his wait. Scott followed the Lord's leading to a new doctor, and finally, the unknown was known: Scott was diagnosed with rheumatoid arthritis.

THIS PRINCIPLE IN YOUR PAUSE

Now it's your turn. Use the "Worth the Wait" pages in chapter 10 to examine your current wait in light of the lessons outlined in this chapter.

Here are some prompts to help you get started:

Who has God unexpectedly brought into your life to help you as you wait?

How have they helped? If you feel abandoned, like nobody cares, ask God to help you recognize and accept the help He wants to give.

Digging Deeper with David: Psalm 52

Read Psalm 52.

Ahimelek was the priest in Nob and the second priest to help David out of a tough spot. He was more than the priest of Nob to David; Ahimelek helped save David. But this act of bravery turned out to be more than a risk. Let's get a little backstory.

Jealousy had totally consumed Saul. He hunted David like a wild animal, determined more than ever to get rid of him once and for all. After receiving provisions from Ahimelek, David regrouped in the cave of Adullam and found safekeeping for his parents in Moab (1 Sam. 22:2–4). He decided to return to Judah, where he learned Saul and his armies were searching the countryside to find and kill him.

The hot pursuit brought Saul to stop and rest. Doeg, the chief shepherd, entered the scene and reported all that he had seen occur between Ahimelek and David. In a rage, Saul ordered Ahimelek and his entire family to be executed.

Psalm 52 is David's response to the tragedy that occurred in Nob following Ahimelek's act of courage. David was heartbroken over the wickedness.

God brings unexpected people—and allows uninvited ones—into the ebb and flow of our wait. As the wait tarries, it's easy to grow cynical and influenced by others both positively and negatively. We have to stay close to God so through the Holy Spirit we recognize wrong influences.

Read 1 Corinthians 15:33.

Fill in the blanks: _____ company corrupts good _____.

BAD COMPANY PROMOTES SELF RATHER THAN GOD

Doeg was bad company in every sense of the word. He taunted Saul with the news of David's help from Ahimelek, and he made himself the "go-to guy" in the situation. Self-promoters have a lot of knowledge, or at least act like it, in order to seem indispensable. These people are the worst kind of bad company because their only goal is to elevate themselves.

Read 1 Corinthians 10:31.

What should we do for the glory or promotion of self? _____
_____

Humility is a characteristic we learn through in-the-moment practice. The more we deflect our "self," the more we reflect Him. In true God-style, He will then bless our obedience in ways greater than we could ever imagine.

Read 1 Peter 5:6.

What happens to the humble?
_____

BAD COMPANY SPEAKS UGLY RATHER THAN LOVELY

When my children were young and got a little sassy around my mother-in-law, she would say, "Don't talk ugly." Children are much easier to train and teach than grown-ups. It's easier to replace ugly talk with lovely talk from the mouth of a child than the mouth of an adult.

Read Psalm 52:2–4.

How did David describe an ugly talker?

_____

_____

As we wait, our faith can wane. God seems inactive and our commitment to the study of God's Word doesn't seem to be paying off. This makes our resistance low and our heart susceptible to bad company. Maybe you return to an old stomping ground. Perhaps you tune in to the television show you once watched *just to see* what's happening.

We need God's Word when our faith is weak as much as we need it when our faith is strong. What we put in our heart will eventually come out of our mouth (Luke 6:45).

The antidote for ugly talk is found Ephesians 4:29. How does lovely talk differ from ugly talk?

_____

_____

BAD COMPANY LOVES EVIL RATHER THAN GOOD

Scripture says Doeg plotted destruction (Ps. 52:2). Bad-company people have a heart to hurt, rather than help, others. While Saul's other men refused to kill Ahimelek and his family, Doeg didn't hesitate. Evil breeds evil. Good begets good.

I AM AN OLIVE TREE

While we wait, even on the hardest days, even when we don't *feel* like it, we have to do everything possible to keep our faith strong. Can we be olive trees?

I don't like olives, and I knew very little about them when I first started studying David's works, but when David claimed to be one, I was intrigued. An olive tree is strong and lives a long time. When fruitful and cared for, an olive tree can live up to a thousand years! They are known as a symbol of joy, peace, and happiness. I'm not interested in living a thousand years (at least not on this side of heaven), but I love the thought of being fruitful.

Read Psalm 52:8.

How did David flourish?

_____

An olive tree will flourish only when it is planted in the right climate, receives the right nutrients, and has the right amount of water. It is completely dependent on its caregiver, but with expert care and nutrients, an olive tree will produce an abundant crop. The same can be said of God's children. God is our expert caregiver. This is something David learned, and like David, we can flourish and be fruitful because of the great attention God gives us as we trust in His unfailing love.

7

When Waiting Encounters the Uninvited

Meeting new and unexpected people can make our wait more pleasant, not to mention more tolerable. I love how God uses these surprising guests, and Himself, to strengthen our faith! However, the unexpected people aren't the only ones who may accompany us on our journey. Without our knowledge or consent, the *Uninviteds* often highjack a ride. These interlopers interfere with the positive and progressive work the Holy Spirit desires to accomplish. Their goal? To sabotage and suffocate our faith.

In previous chapters, we've talked about different battles we face as we wait. Now let's dive deeper into three specific battles we are likely to encounter. David went to war with these uninvited trouble-makers: depression, discouragement, and doubt. A few verses reveal how he was gripped by these three *D*s:

How long, LORD? Will you forget me forever?
> How long will you hide your face from me?
How long must I wrestle with my thoughts
> and day after day have sorrow in my heart?
> How long will my enemy triumph over me?
>> (Ps. 13:1–2)

My tears have been my food
> day and night,
while people say to me all day long,
> "Where is your God?" (Ps. 42:3)

See how they lie in wait for me!
> Fierce men conspire against me
> for no offense or sin of mine, LORD.
I have done no wrong, yet they are ready to attack
> me.
> Arise to help me; look on my plight!
>> (Ps. 59:3–4)

Look and see, there is no one at my right hand;
> no one is concerned for me.
I have no refuge;
> no one cares for my life. (Ps. 142:4)

We've all been there. When our wait seems like it will never end, we encounter *Uninvited Depression* and cry out to God, "How long, Lord? How long will You hide Your face from me?" We catch our breath only to bump into *Uninvited Discouragement* crouching around the next bend, waiting to steal our peace. With our cage still rattled, we come face to face with *Uninvited Doubt* that is eager to fill our mind with untruth.

The *Uninviteds.* They are deceitful, cunning, and don't act alone. These intruders are merely puppets on a string; they are used as weapons of war against us by their puppet master, Satan. He is our enemy, whose sole mission is to steal, kill, and destroy the abundant life Jesus died to give (John 10:10).

There's no need to dread or fear the *Uninviteds*, though. We can take heart and claim victory over them: "No weapon forged against you will prevail, and you will refute every tongue that accuses you" (Isa. 54:17). Underline the words *forged against*. Isaiah didn't say a weapon *would not* come against us. He emphatically proclaimed a weapon would not prosper *when* it is forged against us. The enemy is aggressive and relentless. He has a plethora of weapons in his arsenal, but God will defeat each and every one. Bible commentator David Guzik illuminated Isaiah 54:17:

> The LORD will not allow the weapon formed against His servants to prosper. Sometimes this means the LORD takes the weapon out of the hand of the enemy of His servants. Sometimes it means that God allows the weapon to strike, but brings a greater good out of it than the pain of the imme-diate blow. In allowing this, God will not allow the weapon to prosper, but transforms the violent sword into a trowel for building His kingdom.[13]

The enemy wants to stop, or at least thwart, the building process. He sends the *Uninviteds* to mess with us. In order to stay present in the present, and to maintain God's peace in His pauses and plans, we might have to wrestle with the *Uninviteds*. To defeat them, we must recognize their presence and know how to go to war.

RECOGNIZING THE UNINVITEDS

The *Uninviteds* relentlessly pursued David most of his life. As we wait, our mind is invaded by the same *Uninviteds* that harassed David; we fight the same enemy who uses the same old tired tactics. Such warring causes our body to become weak and our spirit to waver. Worn out physically and spiritually, our mind is then easily susceptible to these troublemakers.

Our mind is the battlefield where the *Uninviteds* wage war. They march over the terrain of our past to depress us. Then they parade over the fields of our present to discourage us. Lastly, they trample over the landscape of our future to create doubt. When our peace turns to anxiety, joy to sorrow, and laughter to crying, we know the *Uninviteds* have inserted themselves in our wait. We will go deeper into warring strategies later in this chapter, but for now let's talk defense.

Peter, one of Jesus's right-hand men, summed up the best way to defend our mind when he wrote, "Wherefore gird up the loins of your mind, be sober, and hope to the end for the grace that is to be brought unto you at the revelation of Jesus Christ" (1 Pet. 1:13 KJV). Now, I realize "gird up the loins" is not twenty-first-century lingo, but hang in there with me.

Typical attire for first-century Jews was a long tunic worn over a girdle or loincloth. When the need arose to move quickly and freely, people would pull the longer part of the tunic up between their legs and tuck it into their belt. This was referred to as "girding up your loins." Pause and snap a picture of this mental image.

Peter's metaphorical message is to take care of our mind by tying down every thought and emotion with biblical truth so that we can fully hope in the grace of God. We often clog our thoughts with wrong thinking and emotional entanglements, which leads us to depression, discouragement, and doubt. Our safeguard against these is to know and yield to God's Word. Each day, we have to gird up our mind with Scripture and tuck it in with truth.

This all sounds good in theory, right? Yet sometimes it's difficult to keep our thoughts tucked into the truth, and instead we end up tripping over the lies and doubt. Do you respond to mind battles as I do? *I'm not strong enough. I can't do this. It's too hard. I don't know the Bible. I've tried to read and understand it, but I can't. I'm just not disciplined or smart enough.*

Take heart! You can do this. It's not too hard. Through the power of the Holy Spirit, you are disciplined (2 Tim. 1:7). We have the power of the risen Lord living in our heart. He has given us a mind to understand what He reveals in Scripture. Let's gird up our thoughts with truth and ready ourselves to recognize and battle the *Uninviteds*.

THEY MARCH TO OUR PAST: DEPRESSION

What would you consider your greatest achievement? A happy family, satisfying job, or comfortable home? Maybe running a marathon, finishing a quilt, growing prize-winning rose bushes, or surviving cancer? Personal achievements can often dull us to a false sense of security and self-sufficiency. These are all mind lies from the enemy. One particular achievement far exceeds any other: living to the fullest the life God planned for you.

You see, the enemy wants to distract us with the lie that we can achieve peace and happiness on our own and that these things will fulfill us. Once we recognize that these things can't sustain our joy, the enemy will try to block us from living fully for God. We may feel gloomy, thinking nothing else will fulfill us the way a full nest, active lifestyle, or busy job would. Take note of that slump, and take time to lean into God. *Uninvited Depression* is often a prequel to your greatest achievement. That's why the great Bible teacher Charles Spurgeon once said, "Before any great achievement, some measure of depression is very usual."

We are hard pressed to find the actual word *depression* in the most commonly used Bible translations. Synonyms such as *forlorn, downhearted, troubled,* and *brokenhearted* are there, but rarely the word *depression.* However, people who battled with it are mentioned throughout Scripture. Our shepherd-soon-to-be-king was just one of many who fought this *Uninvited.*

- Job: "My heart is broken. Depression haunts my days" (Job 30:16 TLB).
- Hannah: "I am a woman who is deeply troubled.... I have been praying here out of my great anguish and grief" (1 Sam. 1:15–16).
- Nehemiah: "So the king said to me, 'Why are you sad, when you aren't sick? This is nothing

but depression.' I was overwhelmed with fear"
(Neh. 2:2 HCSB).

- David: "Have mercy on me, O God, according to
your unfailing love; according to your great compassion blot out my transgressions" (Ps. 51:1).

Depression can be birthed out of myriad places. Job experienced
the sudden loss of his family and wealth. Hannah wrestled for years
with an unfulfilled dream of being a mother. Nehemiah battled
with anxiety because his beloved Israel lay in ruins after Babylonian
captivity. David lived with the unconfessed sins of his affair with
Bathsheba and the murder of her husband. *Uninvited Depression*
attacked everywhere then, and it wages war everywhere today. It
doesn't discriminate because of age, race, nationality, sex, or religion.

Though I have experienced sadness in my life, I haven't personally brawled with this *Uninvited*. However, I have been an eyewitness
to the wounds it inflicts. As mentioned earlier, my daughter battled
with depression in middle school, and it wasn't until her senior year
in high school that she began to experience freedom.

Blaire's fight ended when she followed the wise counsel of Peter. She
girded her mind with God's Word. She became a student of Scripture
and saw its connection to everyday life. In moments of weakness, she
chose to yield to the truth she had learned, even if she didn't *feel* like
it. This wasn't an easy wait or quick fix. Overcoming depression takes
patience, tremendous mental vigor, and discipline. Each day she had
to make the decision to tuck in her tunic and war with her enemy.

Depression has varying degrees, some being more serious than
others. I am not claiming *girding up* is a cure-all for everyone;

sometimes other measures are needed in addition to Scripture. In some cases, exercise, changing our diet, or simply a shift in our schedule to create some white space relieves stress. If you are battling depression and have not found relief through lifestyle changes, prayer, and reading the Word, please know that many godly counselors are available to listen and steer you in a healing direction. Contact your church office or ask a friend who has gone to a therapist for a recommendation. Some seasons of depression are situational and pass in time; others may need the benefit of additional support such as counseling or medication to overcome.

You are wholly and dearly loved. God's desire is for you to live fully in this truth. In the wait of healing and victory, allow Paul's words in 2 Corinthians 4:8–9 to regenerate hope: "We have troubles all around us, but we are not defeated. We do not know what to do, but we do not give up the hope of living. We are persecuted, but God does not leave us. We are hurt sometimes, but we are not destroyed" (NCV).

Job, Hannah, Nehemiah, and David each experienced depression as a prequel to his or her greatest achievement. Job lost everything prior to confessing his pride to God and having all his earthly riches restored. Hannah faithfully prayed for a child. The Lord heard her prayer, and when Samuel was born, she dedicated him to the Lord's service. Samuel grew up to become a prophet to God's people. Nehemiah's depression was followed by the rebuilding of Jerusalem. David became the greatest king in Israel's history. In addition to earthly achievements, these amazing people realized the ultimate achievement: living the life God designed for them. All four defeated the enemy's attempt to march to their past in order to steal their peace.

THEY PARADE OVER OUR PRESENT: DISCOURAGEMENT

Discouragement is an intruder I have battled for years. I echo the words of Billy Graham, who said, "The Christian life is not a constant high. I have my moments of deep discouragement. I have to go to God in prayer with tears in my eyes, and say, 'O God, forgive me,' or 'Help me.'"

This *Uninvited* has two first cousins—*Negativity* and *Rejection*—who have also bullied me as long as I can remember. From the time I was a young girl, they whispered, "You know you will not make the team, so don't even try. Don't put yourself out there. You will fail, and everyone will know." And when I mustered up the courage to attempt something and failed, *Discouragement* sarcastically muttered, "See, I told you so."

These intruders hung around in the shadows of my adulthood and seized any confidence maturity might have given me. They were the roots of my anger when I called my daughter the horrible name, as I mentioned earlier. Their constant repetition of "You're not good enough" drove a wedge between my husband and me. They overshadowed my enthusiasm and made me feel unworthy to serve in ministry. I hated them yet never fought against them. In a weird sort of way, these familiar sojourners were like family. My job was to put up with them. Then one day, I decided to *gird up*.

The admission of my need marked the beginning of my healing.

Like Billy Graham, and perhaps like you, I went to God in tears and cried, "Help me, Lord!" The admission of my need marked the beginning of my healing. The Lord led me to the best place of healing: Himself, through His Word. At the age of thirty-four, I began to open my Bible on days other than Sundays. Early on, Psalm 1 grabbed my heart.

> Blessed is the one
> > who does not walk in step with the wicked
> or stand in the way that sinners take
> > or sit in the company of mockers,
> but whose delight is in the law of the LORD,
> > and who meditates on his law day and night.
> That person is like a tree planted by streams of water,
> > which yields its fruit in season
> and whose leaf does not wither—
> > whatever they do prospers. (vv. 1–3)

The psalmist's words became my personal prayer. *Help me stay planted by the streams of Your water, God. Keep me from wickedness. Help me meditate on Your law day and night.* Oh, how I longed to delight in God rather than wallow with *Discouragement*.

Every day started in His Word. Most days I didn't understand what I read, but I believed in God's faithfulness, and I noticed how Bible verses started to repeat in my head more than *Discouragement's* voice. Determined to stay refreshed by God's Word, like a tree planted by streams of water, I started to keep a Bible always within arm's reach: in the car, beside my bed, on the end table by the couch, in the kitchen. At one point, I had verses taped on nearly every doorframe in my house. I'm not sharing this to make myself sound superspiritual. I'm sharing this to show how desperate I was to defeat *Discouragement*, *Negativity*, and *Rejection*.

My victory has taken years to realize. The battle has been slow, but every time I read and meditate on Scripture, I gain ground. Every now and then, *Discouragement* sets a trap; however, with God's wisdom, I am able to avoid it. I shout my victory chant, "No weapon formed against me will prosper." The bullies flee. I praise. Why don't you shout the victory chant aloud right now? Go ahead. I'll wait.

David dealt with criticism from his wife and negativity from his brothers, but he didn't allow *Discouragement* to defeat him. He stayed close to God, and he cried out every time he needed help. We are blessed to be able to cry out to God for help and search His Word for inspiration.

Sometimes the totality and enormity of God's Word can be overwhelming. Have you ever felt this way? You know encouragement will come from Scripture, but when you open the Bible, you don't know how to find the encouragement that awaits. When I have this feeling, I create my own mini-Bible. Using my Bible's concordance, I look up a word that has something to do with my current state of mind and circumstances. For example, if I am feeling rejected, I find the word *love* and look up verses about God's love. Then, in a small spiral-bound notebook, I record every verse that lifts my heart. This mini-Bible becomes my go-to place for quick encouragement.

God was faithful to David. God will be faithful to you and me as well.

THEY TRAMPLE OVER OUR FUTURE: DOUBT

The greatest defense against *Uninvited Doubt* is to focus on the hope we have in God. Focusing on *Doubt* is like walking amid the funhouse mirrors at the carnival. Small is big. Big is bigger. Nothing is as it seems. *Doubt* will trample over our future and cause us to miss God's miracles. I like the way Henry Drummond put it: "Christ never failed to distinguish between doubt and unbelief. Doubt is can't believe. Unbelief is won't believe. Doubt is honesty. Unbelief is obstinacy. Doubt is looking for light. Unbelief is content with darkness."

Doubt is ambiguous. It will cause us to question what we know to be true about God. *If God really loves me, then why am I still waiting? If His plan is really perfect, then why do I have to experience such pain?* Oh, friend, don't fall for *Doubt*. Stand firm in the truth of Isaiah 59:1: "Surely the arm of the LORD is not too short to save, nor his ear too dull to hear."

God hears you. God can reach you. God does love you. His plans may bring pain, but not without purpose. He is trustworthy. He works everything out for your good and His glory, even if that requires a little sheep tending.

> **Doubt will tread over our future and
> cause us to miss God's miracles.**

The *Uninviteds* magnify the circumstances of our wait. Until we defeat these unwelcomed guests, they will continue to march across the pages of our story. Jesus paid too high a price for us to succumb to *Depression*, *Discouragement*, and *Doubt*. They must go!

RIDDING OURSELVES OF THE UNINVITEDS

We've seen that the *Uninviteds* are controlled by the puppet master Satan, our real enemy. Satan is a spiritual being, an angel created by

God, who tried to usurp God's authority. His pride caused him to be thrown out of heaven, yet he is ruler of this world (Isa. 14:12–15; 2 Cor. 4:4). Our battle isn't against flesh and blood; our conflict is spiritual. Therefore, we must *war* with all our spiritual might.

War is defined as active hostility and contention between two parties. Take note of the word *active*. Satan's attacks are active, so we must be active. Jesus said of Satan in John 10:10, "The thief's purpose is to steal and kill and destroy" (NLT). Peter described Satan as a prowling lion looking for someone to devour. He warned us to be sober and alert (1 Pet. 5:8). As a lion won't stop until he consumes his prey, so Satan won't stop until *Depression*, *Discouragement*, and *Doubt* overcome us. He is on a mission to keep us from trusting God's Word and yielding to God's ways.

To achieve victory, we need to write our plan of war and strategize against the enemy. We are active warriors who need a battle plan. I like to use the acronym WAR: willing, armed, and right minded.

WILLING

My willingness to finally defeat the *Uninviteds* was directly related to my level of misery. *Miserable* is the perfect word to describe my spirit when I started meditating on Scripture day and night. In my morning meditation, I was introduced to David and his misery. His desperate words in Psalm 51:12 struck a chord with my heartstrings: "Restore to me the joy of your salvation and grant me a willing spirit, to sustain me."

I took his prayer and made it my own. In addition to my planted-by-streams prayer, I began to pray the willing-spirit prayer.

Lord, restore to me the joy of Your salvation. Give me a willing spirit to obey You.

As wonderful as praying Scripture was, the *Uninviteds* still attacked me. I tried to defend myself against them by repeating truths and praying, but I sensed God wanted me to take another step to ensure victory. I'd naively taken my misery and desperation to God, expecting Him to *fix this* or *change that*. Yet I never gave a second thought to my participation in the process. We need Him, and He needs our willingness. When I started praying my willing-spirit prayer, I began to have such a spirit (slowly, but surely).

When I first began praying Psalm 51:12, I was more than willing to let God help me, but I was less than willing to cooperate with Him. One area in particular I needed to change in order to slay the *Uninviteds* was not watching a certain television show. (I know. Clearly I have an issue with the television.) But I couldn't see how changing the channel at 9:00 p.m. every Thursday would make a difference in my battle against *Discouragement*.

My favorite television shows involve crime solving. For years, I faithfully watched a program that combined crime, law, and humor. A unique combination, right? I thought so, and I argued with God that my misery didn't stem from my enjoying a late-night drama. After all, the show didn't *discourage* me per se and I had already given up one show. Watching this seemed harmless; however, I sensed a conviction from the Lord to stop tuning in each week. Notice I said "*sensed* a conviction from the Lord," not "was *clearly directed* by the Lord." So I chose not to submit.

Ignoring this conviction broke my fellowship with God. The desire to be with Him wasn't as strong as it once had been, and when

I did spend time with Him, I allowed myself to become distracted and impatient. It was just a television show to me, but to God it was a test of my willingness to cooperate with His work to eliminate life invaders that sought to steal my peace.

At times, the Lord will ask us to lay aside or forgo a pleasure (even a harmless one) in order to gird our mind. Watching this show diluted my thoughts; I focused more on the plot than Scripture. This left my defenses down, and I wasn't ready to jump into action to defend myself against the *Uninviteds*. I wanted God to snap His fingers and do all the work for me, but I soon recognized that I had to be willing to do my part too. The *fixing of this* and the *changing of that* involve the *surrendering of me*.

The work of surrender is challenging, but the rewards are worth it. With God, the dividends exceed the cost. The more we surrender and act out of a willing spirit, the greater the power we will experience with God. Victory comes when we are willing and well-armed warriors.

ARMED

For armor fashion tips, we will turn to none other than our what-to-wear-to-battle resident expert, the apostle Paul. Paul wasn't a soldier; he was a prisoner. But his close and personal contact with Roman soldiers gave him firsthand knowledge of how to dress for battle. This fashion combination is everyday attire, not just for special occasions. In following his expertise described in Ephesians 6, we can dress appropriately each day to successfully engage and defeat our enemy and his minions.

The Belt of Truth

This refers to the application of God's Word in our life. Being doers of the Word, not just hearers, helps us maintain a strong relationship with God. Just as a belt helped Roman soldiers hold everything in place, God's Word enables us to hold our thoughts and emotions in alignment with truth. Each day as we spend time reading and studying the Bible, we are securing ourselves with truth.

The Breastplate of Righteousness

Roman soldiers anchored their breastplates to their belts and wore them to protect their hearts. Likewise, we cover our emotions and actions with righteousness—rightness with God. Through Jesus's death, we are made right with God, our sins are forgiven, and we are given Jesus's righteousness as our own. Protecting and maintaining our heart's purity demonstrates our respect to God for giving His only Son for the sake of our righteousness.

Shoes of Readiness Fitted with the Gospel of God's Peace

Soldiers' shoes were spiked to help maintain balance. God's peace enables us to remain mentally steady as we walk through the uneven terrain of life. Living at peace with those who don't desire to live at peace with us is challenging. God's Word says, "If it is possible, as far as it depends on you, live at peace with everyone" (Rom. 12:18). "*If* it is possible." We aren't responsible for the outcome. We are responsible only for making the effort. Our efforts are vital to securing our peace in His pauses.

Shield of Faith

The shield guarded the soldiers against arrows. We hold our faith up to shield ourselves against the arrows of corruption and seduction of the world. Standing up for injustices and responding to the cries of the needy with the love of Christ is the way to lead the world out of darkness. Often arrows of injustice and hurt are hurled at us during our wait. With our shield of faith we can repel painful arrows.

Helmet of Salvation

Soldiers wore helmets to protect their heads. Our salvation in Jesus and knowledge of His Word protect our mind from the enemy's attempts to attack us with untruth and doubt. Just as a football player puts on a helmet to protect his head and proudly display his team's logo, each day we must put on our helmet to show the world whose team we are on. The enemy can't steal our salvation, but a wait can cause us to doubt it. Let's keep our helmet buckled securely around our chin to prevent doubt from creeping in.

Sword of the Spirit

Commonly, double-edged swords were Roman soldiers' chosen weapons for attacking. The writer of Hebrews referred to God's Word, our sword of the Spirit, as a double-edged sword, dividing soul and spirit, joints and marrow; it judges the thoughts and attitudes of the heart (4:12). God uses His Word to teach, rebuke, correct, and train.

But He can't do the work He desires to do in our life unless we open His book each day and apply what we learn.

Each day we are tempted to be drawn into the drama of the world around us. Social media stirs up negativity. Our office can be a breeding ground for unwholesome conversation. Most prime-time television shows and movies contradict the values of our faith. Donning ourselves with the armor of God makes us less vulnerable to the pull of the world and empowers us to be fruitful in our waiting days.

RIGHT MINDED

Waging war against the *Uninviteds* can be tricky. Our enemy strategizes to take us down any way he can. One main way is to cunningly attack our thoughts. In chapter 5, we learned the effectiveness of making our negative thoughts bow to the truth (2 Cor. 10:5). Now we will learn how Scripture can help us redirect wrong thinking. Because wrong thinking leads to wrong action, the *Uninviteds'* aim is to turn a right-minded thinker into a wrong-minded casualty. In Philippians 4:8, Paul taught a right-minded battle strategy that cannot fail: "Finally, brothers and sisters, whatever is true, whatever is noble, whatever is right, whatever is pure, whatever is lovely, whatever is admirable—if anything is excellent or praiseworthy—think about such things."

How is that for a counterattack to *Depression*, *Discouragement*, and *Doubt*? Highlight *true, noble, right, pure, lovely, admirable, excellent*, and *praiseworthy*. We protect our mind and maintain peace when we park on these positive truths. Words such as *false, lowly, wrong, fake, ugly, unworthy, insignificant*, and *disliked* bring us down. This is stinkin' thinkin', and it has got to go!

Replacing Satan's worn-out lies with God's Word always defeats wrong-minded thinking. As we dress each day, let's tuck our thinking cap under our helmet of salvation and filter every thought through Scripture.

WHEN WARRING MAKES US WEARY

Let's face it, even when we have a willing spirit, are wearing our battle gear, and are right minded, winning the war against the *Uninviteds* can take time. Our wait can become a lonely place. We initially engage in battle with confidence, and we fight every weapon forged against us. We believe in victory, but as the battle rages on, spiritual warfare tires us. Our spirit is willing, but our flesh weakens. Often, those who have been holding our arms become fatigued; prayers dwindle, comforting calls fizzle out, and we discover we are alone and left to self-soothe.

David self-soothed. He penned many of his greatest psalms while rejected and alone. Earlier in this chapter, we read some verses David wrote while facing the *Uninviteds*. To demonstrate the power of self-soothing, or crying out to God in hope of comfort, let's look at verses at the end of those psalms. For David, pouring out his pain delivered him to a place of praise.

> But I trust in your unfailing love;
>> my heart rejoices in your salvation.
> I will sing the Lord's praise,
>> for he has been good to me.
>>> (Ps. 13:5–6)

Why, my soul, are you downcast?
> Why so disturbed within me?
Put your hope in God,
for I will yet praise him,
> my Savior and my God. (Ps. 42:11)

But I will sing of your strength,
> in the morning I will sing of your love;
for you are my fortress,
> my refuge in times of trouble.

You are my strength, I sing praise to you;
> you, God, are my fortress,
> my God on whom I can rely. (Ps. 59:16–17)

Set me free from my prison,
> that I may praise your name.
Then the righteous will gather about me
> because of your goodness to me. (Ps. 142:7)

The *Uninviteds'* ultimate goal is to sabotage and suffocate our faith. Through Christ, we have the equipment and the ability to keep *Depression*, *Discouragement*, and *Doubt* from being victorious. We gird up and dress for success in the armor of God. When these saboteurs show up to wreak havoc in our thought life, we wield our mini-Bible, command them to flee, and soothe ourselves with comfort only God's Word can provide. Though unpleasant, our experiences with the *Unexpecteds* and *Uninviteds* train us to wait well.

THIS PRINCIPLE IN THEIR PAUSE

Ashley journeyed out in the beginning of her calling with bold-ness and excitement. Along the way, bitterness replaced boldness, apathy replaced excitement, and she had thoughts of giving up altogether. The more she focused on what others had accom-plished instead of how far God had brought her, the more she began to sink into depression, discouragement, and doubt. It was a wearying cycle. Challenging herself to live out Scripture, going deeper in prayer, and learning to preach to her soul during times of enemy attack were the only ways that she was able to stand firm.

Samantha learned early on in her wait how slippery the slope into the quicksand of discouragement could be. To help her stay out of it, she set up "guardrails" by answering her questioning doubts with truth.

Question: What if I never get married?

Answer: My greatest good and deepest joy is Jesus, not a hus-band. So if I never get married, I still have all I need.

Question: What if I am always alone?

Answer: God is with me and will never leave me.

Question: Does being single mean I am not worthy of being loved?

Answer: God loves me with an everlasting love.

And if she went beyond those guardrails, down the slippery slope, she recalled this verse: "When I said, 'My foot is slipping,' your unfailing love, LORD, supported me. When anxiety was great within me, your consolation brought me joy" (Ps. 94:18–19).

Dianna had to fight against the pull to stay under the covers. Her sheets had a literal face impression in them. Every day was filled with an uninvited "something." This depression was not natural or welcome. Instead of the depressing turning dramatic, she was determined to find laughter in the yuck. She sought to live out Proverbs 31:25–26: "She is clothed with strength and dignity, and she laughs without fear of the future. When she speaks, her words are wise, and she gives instructions with kindness" (NLT).

Our story: As Scott's diagnosis sank in, we faced all the *Uninviteds* at once. I was mad at God for me making me go through this. *Why would You not heal my mother and then allow the very same disease to strike my husband? You could've stopped this and You didn't. I watched her suffer, and now I get to watch him suffer. Really, God?* In addition to the diagnosis, Scott walked through an unexpected professional change. The combination of these major crises at the same time sent him into a deep depression. Our wait was over, but were we just moving into another one?

THIS PRINCIPLE IN YOUR PAUSE

Now it's your turn. Use the "Worth the Wait" pages in chapter 10 to examine your current wait in light of the lessons outlined in this chapter.

Here are some prompts to help you get started:

Consider how the *Uninviteds* have intruded in your story.

How are you willing, armed, and right minded?

What can you do to strengthen your warfare?

Digging Deeper with David: Psalm 54

Read Psalm 54.

Imagine sitting at work and doing your job when out of nowhere you notice a spear coming toward your head. Instinct takes over; you duck and run. Fearing for his life, David ran to Michal, his wife, and hid. Saul, in relentless pursuit, stationed troops outside his house with orders to kill David (1 Sam. 19). With Michal's help, though, David escaped by climbing out the window.

I wonder how often I have narrowly escaped the grasp of my enemy—or how close I have come to defeat but was kept safe because of God's presence. Whether the enemy is an actual person or a threat to our mind, we can be confident in God's protection.

Read Psalm 139:7–12.

What do these verses tell us about God's watchful care?

_____

From the moment he received his anointing until his death, David enjoyed very little peace. He knew the agony of defeat, the pain of betrayal, and the deception of being double-crossed. On the run again from Saul, he moved his army to the wilderness of the En Gedi. And like countless times before, he turned to his great God.

Read Psalm 54:1–2.

David asked God for three things. Name them.

_____

_____

Read Psalm 54:5.

David prayed about his enemies. What did he ask God?

_____

_____

On more than one occasion, I have prayed a "Help, God" prayer. *Save me. Clear my name. Hear my prayer.* This may disappoint you, but I have also prayed a similar "Get 'em, God" prayer concerning my enemies. *Get them, God, like they got me!* Admitting such a thing is a bit embarrassing, but it opens the door for a discussion about dealing with our enemies.

WHO IS MY ENEMY?

We can't have a healthy discussion about enemies unless we have a good working definition of *enemy*. To help, let's answer the questions below. This is a good review from our chapter.

Read 1 Peter 5:8.

Who is our real enemy?

_____

Read John 10:10.

What is the goal of our enemy?

_____

_____

Satan has waged war on God's children. We discussed at great length in the chapter how to WAR against the unseen warriors of the evil one. But how should we respond to those who war against us in the flesh?

HOW SHOULD I TREAT MY ENEMY?

Satan is not our only enemy, unfortunately. At one time or another, we each have faced an enemy with flesh and bones. David faced Saul. Nehemiah faced Tobiah and Sanballat. Paul faced Christian haters. Even Jesus was confronted by adversaries. Jesus's thoughts about enemies are quite different from David's prayers concerning his enemies. Let's hear from Jesus.

Read Luke 6:35.

Name the four things Jesus says we should do for our enemy.

_____

_____

Can we all agree that there are some verses we wish we didn't know about? This verse should come with a warning label: "Impossible Apart from the Holy Spirit." I have to admit it's a lot easier to pray my "Get 'em, God" prayer. But it's important we fully understand what Jesus is asking. Brace yourself.

Love:	to welcome, to be fond of
Do good:	do right so there is not room for blame
Bless:	speak well of, praise
Pray:	to make an earnest petition

In the flesh, Jesus's instructions are not possible, but we have the Holy Spirit to enable us to accomplish the impossible. And Jesus isn't asking us to do anything He didn't do while on earth. Consider His relationship with Judas. Jesus knew Judas was going to betray Him, yet He loved, did good, blessed, and prayed for him.

See John 13. What did Jesus do for *all* His disciples? _____

_____

A few years ago, I was deeply betrayed by several people I thought were my friends. *How could they have done such a thing? Why would they say such things? I thought we were friends.* The pain ran deep.

Like David, I took my agony to my great God. I committed to pray about the situation, though I did a fair amount of complaining too (I never claimed to be a super-Christian!). I prayed for those involved but mostly from my head. Over time, the prayers moved from my head to my heart. Prayer brought healing. Eventually, I had opportunities to do good, and now, years later, I am able to bless.

Love, do good, pray, and bless as God leads. These are His directions for peaceful living. When we follow His directions, there will always be blessings.

8

When Waiting Turns into a Wilderness Experience

It is easy to stay strong and wait well for a while. Working out our salvation keeps us busy, and tending to sheep occupies our mind … for a short time. But as weeks turn into months, and months stretch into years, we tire of waiting. Temporary pauses are more palatable than extended stays. I get antsy when my wait exceeds my limits of acceptability. Sometimes I get more than antsy as I continue to battle with the *Uninviteds*, as we talked about in our previous chapter. How about you?

Admitting I become restless and down when my wait takes longer than I desire doesn't make me feel bad. I'm not alone in feeling this way. David had trouble waiting patiently too. In anguish, he cried out to the Lord four times, "How long?" (Ps. 13:1–2). I can almost hear his plea echo across the valleys in which he ran to escape Saul. His eyes were on the palace, yet he was still stuck in a pasture. Like David's, our wait can begin to feel more like a wilderness experience than an exhilarating adventure. Before we know it, our soul is panting and our body is weak.

Temporary pauses are more palatable than extended stays.

The wilderness makes us desperate to end the wait before we are fully equipped to receive what God has prepared for us. In our state of despair, we respond in one of three ways:

- Continue to seek the Lord, work out our salvation, and tend to our sheep.
- "Help" God by manipulating circumstances to rush our desired outcome.
- Turn the object of our wait into an idol.

David chose the first way, and he is an example of staying the course. His wait turned into a life-and-death wilderness experience as he ran from Saul and hid in caves. His psalms reveal his desire to fully understand God's plan as well as his frustration in the wait. His poetic melodies demonstrate trust and faith in God's perfect timing.

Even when he felt abandoned by those he loved and trusted, David never manipulated the circumstances to gain position. And not one psalm even hints of his idolizing the throne and kingship. David waited well, even when the wait became a wilderness.

Our journey together is equipping us to wait well too. We are staying hydrated and strengthened as we deepen our relationship with Jesus, our Living Water (John 7:38) and Bread of Life (John 6:35). We might *feel* abandoned and forgotten by those we love, but the One who loves us most will never leave or forsake us (Heb. 13:5). Here's the truth: how we *feel* is not how it *is*. Perhaps your wilderness has you waiting to be healed from a long-term illness or praying the unemployment checks continue until you get another job. Maybe the bank foreclosed on your house or your aging parents' long-term health issues are taxing on your family life.

Friend, I understand. Sometimes, we think, *If I can only make it to tomorrow!* But the next day is just as hard as the day before. Seasons of waiting can be depleting.

One of my friends is separated from her husband. For nine long months they have not spoken or seen each other. The husband needs a lot of counseling so he can be free and healed from several addictions. It is a safeguard for her heart not to be around him until that happens. Their initial separation was for six weeks. That stretched into three months, then five months, and now they are looking at a year. Each day, she hopes for a phone call from her husband saying he is taking full responsibility for his issues and has committed to pursuing help. But that call hasn't come yet. So every new day, she trudges through her wilderness again. She forces herself out of bed, makes breakfast for her daughter, and goes to work. My friend waits on the Lord and waits on her husband to take the right steps to restore their marriage.

Have you been or are you currently in a similar situation? Maybe you are longing for your child to come back to the Lord, or you need to heal, or you are praying for hope in your own marriage. Let's look again at Paul's comforting words of truth, which contrast emotions with reality: "We are hard pressed on every side, but not crushed; perplexed, but not in despair; persecuted, but not abandoned; struck down, but not destroyed" (2 Cor. 4:8–9).

Draw a square around every *but* in the quote, and then underline the phrase behind it. Now lay down your pen and put your hands up and praise the Lord. The wilderness might make us *feel* pressed in, perplexed, persecuted, and struck down, but God is bigger than our feelings and circumstances. That's shoutin' good news!

In the desperation of the wilderness, embracing the truth of Philippians 4:8 seems difficult, and we try to rush our desired outcome. God's timing is absolutely trustworthy. And honestly, He doesn't need our help.

HELPING GOD MAKES MATTERS WORSE

Am I the only one who has tried to assist God in doing His job? When will I ever learn that my "helping" just messes things up and prolongs my waiting? We attempt to lend God a hand because the enemy has whipped up a frenzied, fast-paced culture that has conditioned us to feel we should get what we want when we want it. He's lied by telling us that if the desire of our heart is delayed, we should expedite God's plan by manipulating circumstances to make things happen.

In the wilderness, it's easy to forget our successful attire and mini-Bible. Our once-willing spirit is weary, and our right thinking becomes distorted. We figure that pushing God's agenda ahead of His schedule will shorten our wait. But the enemy has lied, and we have fallen for it hook, line, and sinker. He has been a skilled deceiver for a long time. We're not the only ones he's hoodwinked; he duped Abraham and Sarah, two wonderful people who believed his nonsense.

Abraham and Sarah fell in love and were married. They wanted to have children, but Sarah could not conceive. Decade after decade,

God monitored their desire to be parents. He even visited Abraham and nurtured his parental longings. God told Abraham that someday he would have a son and that all nations on earth would be blessed through him (Gen. 18:18). Sarah and Abraham hoped in this promise, despite a large shadow of doubt looming over their hearts, especially as they passed childbearing age.

The wilderness of the wait became too long for Sarah. She idolized her desire for a child and took matters into her own hands. She *was* going to give her husband a baby, even if it meant she had to help God. Oh, how I wish I could go back in time and give Sarah a reassuring hug and encourage her to press into the promises of God and tell her that her pause was for her good. I can relate to Sarah's deep desire to become a mother and her hurry-it-up mentality. Though I was never tempted to, um, "share" my husband with another woman, I did long to go to great lengths to conceive a child. I was willing to spend large sums of money, go through medical procedures, and travel to specialists.

Sarah convinced Abraham to conceive a child with her maidservant, Hagar. This plan succeeded, and Hagar soon gave birth to Ishmael. This child did not negate God's original plan, though. Approximately fourteen years later, Sarah gave birth to God's promised child, Isaac. At first glance, it sounds like all's well that ends well. Abraham got two sons, one being the promised son. *So what's the big deal if Sarah helped God a little by orchestrating the conception of Ishmael?*

Ishmael was not part of God's plan to bless all nations. Abraham and Sarah's manipulation of God's plan birthed two leaders of two nations. Ishmael became the father of the Ishmaelites with his twelve sons. Isaac became the father of Jacob, who then also fathered twelve sons and was the father of the Israelites. Sounds like a big, happy family, doesn't it? Not exactly. Animosity ran rampant between the descendants of Isaac and Ishmael, and great strife still exists between them. A direct line can be drawn from Isaac to Judaism and Ishmael to Islam.

Manipulating our circumstances to generate the outcome we desire can have kingdom consequences. Our helping God most likely won't result in centuries of fierce and tragic war between two people groups. But it may affect our situation and others in ways we could never guess. Fast-tracking to the object of our wait is never the answer. Let's remember on the hard days that God has a plan for each of us. It's a good plan, a plan worth slowing down for and waiting on. Allow that truth to bring calm to your heart.

WHEN THE OBJECT BECOMES AN IDOL

Sarah wasn't the only person in the Bible who had idol issues. I hear the word *idol*, and my mind races to Exodus 32. I see Aaron crafting a golden calf. More about Aaron later; first, let's talk about the small word with big imagery—*idol*.

Did you have to shift in your seat a little? So did I. The word makes us feel uncomfortable because of the negative connotations it carries. For many years, when I heard teachings on idols and idolatry, I judged and criticized God's chosen people. With my arms folded and a little sass in my attitude, I would shake my head in disbelief that the Israelites, recently rescued out of four hundred years of slavery, turned to a man-made god. However, when I learned the meaning of this small, dangerous word, my attitude waned and my head lowered.

Idolatry is the worship of idols, or excessive devotion or reverence to a person or thing.[14] You might want to take note of that sentence. It's worth remembering. Just because something doesn't look like a golden calf doesn't mean it's not an idol. Anything that replaces God in our heart is an idol.

Those early mornings in my Jesus chair didn't come easy. I loved Jesus with all my heart, but I also loved sleeping with all my heart. Meeting Jesus early meant giving up sleep. Now, I know you might be thinking, *Seriously? Sleep? An idol? But it's necessary and good for you.* Take a look back at the definition of *idolatry* in the previous paragraph. *Excessive devotion.*

I was obsessed with sleep. I chose extra rest over time with the Creator of my time. Sleep competed with the importance of God in my heart, and my actions demonstrated my devotion. That, my friend, is an idol. This truth gets harder to wrap our mind around when the object of our wait affects our very life. God wants us to seek and trust Him to give us all we need, because truly, He is what we need. His peace and hope will carry us through, day by day.

I chose extra rest over time with the Creator of my time.

Replacing the Person of our faith with the object of our wait isn't something we initially set out to do. The waiting wears us down, particularly when we don't continue to seek God. This shifts our focus from the Lord and His grace to the object of our wait. The urge to speed up the process so we can obtain our desired outcome becomes stronger than our will to wait. Aaron and the Israelites felt that urge, and instead of battling it, they succumbed to it.

Following hundreds of years of slavery to the Egyptians, the Israelites found themselves free and wandering the desert on their way to the land God had promised them. They needed guidelines for godly living in this new place. So God invited Moses to climb Mt. Sinai for a little one-on-one time and to receive the Ten Commandments. While Moses communed with God on top of the mountain, he left his brother, Aaron, in charge of the people.

After being without Moses for almost forty days, Aaron and the others became anxious. Not knowing when, or even if, Moses would return, the people begged Aaron to make an idol that could lead them. Under Aaron's command, the people removed their jewelry, threw it into a fire, and Aaron crafted the infamous golden calf. Aaron was skilled as a metal worker and very familiar with a graving tool.[15]

God had shown His mercy, power, and provision in leading the Israelites thus far, yet in the pause, His people forgot His faithfulness. They became impatient. "When the people saw that Moses was so long in coming down from the mountain …" (Exod. 32:1). Does the complaint sound familiar? I know I've said it many times in my wait. *This is taking so long, God!* Impatience leads to irrational thoughts, and it will cause us to make unwise decisions.

So then "they gathered around Aaron and said, 'Come, make us gods who will go before us. As for this fellow Moses who brought us up out of Egypt, we don't know what has happened to him'" (Exod. 32:1). Seasons of "so long" make it easy to elevate what we seek above the God we serve. When our impatience rises, our knees should fall. Hitting our knees in prayer redirects our focus back to God and off the object of our wait.

Pauses are places meant to strengthen our
resolve, not weaken our faith.

In addition to their impatience, the Israelites lacked real commitment to God. Reread Exodus 32:1 and take note of the sarcastic tone: "This Moses guy just up and ditched us. Let's make gods who will actually stick around." They were committed to God as long as there was movement toward the object of their wait (the Promised Land). But when God hit the pause button, their allegiance wavered.

Pauses are places meant to strengthen our resolve, not weaken our faith. The Israelites chose to thoughtlessly throw the plunder from Egypt into the fire to make a false god rather than show their allegiance to God. For those of us on this side of Mt. Sinai, it's easy to point a judgmental finger at the Israelites. But if we're honest, we have a little bit of Abraham, Sarah, and the Israelites hidden within our hurried heart. I know I'm guilty.

For a while, publishing a book was my idol. Nausea sweeps over me even now as I confess this to you. As my sisters in ministry were getting their books published, I whined and my faith waned. Envy consumed me. *Why can't that be me, Lord? She hasn't been serving You as long as I have, and now she is releasing her second book.* It wasn't pretty. Then one day *I* decided *I* was going to write a book.

I informed my family of the changes that would be necessary in order for me to write said book: fewer homemade meals, more chores for them, and less time with me. I threw my family to the wolves, and I threw my words into the fire and crafted an idol in the shape of a book. Tears rim my eyes as I type these words. Instead of strengthening my faith by tending to the sheep in my pasture and working out my salvation, I forged my idol.

Thankfully, before I lost all control, a friend had the courage to speak truth into my heart. "Wendy," she said, "your writing isn't that good, and it really needs a lot of work." Honesty hurts, folks. These words wrapped around my heart like the tentacles of a jellyfish attached to its prey.

I felt the sting of my friend's words. But after some time, I realized she was right and I allowed God to heal me. I laid down my idol and thanked God for a friend who loved me enough to speak truth. My writing wasn't ready to be published, and my heart wasn't ready to receive such a blessing. The pause was my protection.

I joyously resumed my position in my pasture of motherhood. When my daughter called from her room, "Mom, can you make me a 'grilla' cheese sandwich?" (a mispronounced word from her childhood), I responded, "Yes. You want it cut into triangles?" I had the time to make it because I wasn't bowing at the altar of my idol. My husband didn't have to ask if his underwear had gotten lost in the laundry, and watching shows about construction with my son no longer felt like an imposition.

What we are waiting on is too good to hurry!

Day in and day out, God demonstrates His mercy, power, and provision, yet in the pause it is easy to forget His faithfulness. We become impatient and try to rush the wait, especially when life hangs in the balance or our funds have run dry. We often can't wrap our head or heart around God's timing or ways. When our pause seems more like a wilderness, we must be determined to strengthen our faith by trusting His timing. Cling to His peace, and remember— God has a history of working miracles.

SURVIVING THE "HOW LONG?" OF OUR WILDERNESS

I am not an outdoors person. My idea of roughing it is staying in a mountain house without Internet and satellite television. Some of my friends, however, love to camp and are skilled in outdoor survival. When they head out for an adventure, they take rain gear, a first-aid kit, and everything necessary for the trip. If my friends weren't fully trained for survival, elements of the outdoors could be dangerous, even life threatening. The same principle applies to you and me. To remain strong in the wilderness, we must use the skills we have learned in our *wait training*:

- Do what we know to do until we know something else to do.
- Move when God asks.
- Nurture our relations with the Person of our faith through prayer and His Word.
- Accept help from the *Unexpecteds* and defeat the *Uninviteds*.
- Refuse to allow the object of your wait to become an idol.

A stay in the wilderness is inevitable. The wait can be camouflaged as inactivity on God's part. Yet the desolate places are where we experience Him as never before. As we practice our survival skills, God gives us survival assurances.

Survival Assurance #1: God Does Not Ignore My Cries

There are a plethora of examples in Scripture that show how God works in the wilderness and desolate places of our waits, but none is as obvious as when the Israelites left Egypt (before the golden-calf debacle).

Before their exodus, God's people, enslaved under the cruel regime of a new pharaoh, labored beneath the hot sun making bricks. Though generational slavery was a way of life for them and all they knew, they cried out to God for freedom. Yet it seemed to them that God was inactive and unresponsive to their pleas. He was neither.

God had heard their desire to be released, and He provided rescue for them through Moses. The Israelites weren't even aware their liberation was well under way. God is never inactive or unresponsive when it comes to His children. He is always working. "But Jesus replied, 'My Father is always working, and so am I'" (John 5:17 NLT). When God appears to be silent or sedentary, lean closer and press in harder, but never believe He doesn't see or hear your cries.

Our waiting can feel as if it will never end. I imagine that's how the Israelites felt. After four hundred years of waiting for freedom from Egyptian slavery, the Israelites' wait was almost over. Though it seemed He had ignored them, God heard every cry. And He hears your cries too.

"The LORD said, 'I have indeed seen the misery of my people in Egypt. I have heard them crying out because of their slave drivers, and I am concerned about their suffering'" (Exod. 3:7).

In order to change Pharaoh's hard heart and cause him to release the Israelites, God acted on the people's behalf in miraculous ways. He orchestrated armies of locusts, covered the land with frogs, pelted Egypt with hail, and performed seven other plagues. The final plague struck Pharaoh's hard heart. The angel of death took the lives of every firstborn Egyptian child, including Pharaoh's son. In his anguish, Pharaoh made the decision to release God's people. While the Egyptians grieved, the Israelites celebrated their deliverance as Moses led them out of Egypt. It's estimated that more than one million men, women, and children were in the caravan of people who left Egypt.

Survival Assurance #2: God Will Defeat My Enemies

Free! They were finally free! All was well, right? Wrong. Pharaoh realized the impact of his decision to let the Israelites go, gathered his army of 600,000, and set out in hot pursuit to bring them back. He caught up with the Israelites at the edge of the Red Sea. The people saw Pharaoh's army approaching and panic fell upon them. (Cue dramatic music.)

But Moses stretched his hands over the sea, and two walls of water formed, giving the Israelites dry land to walk on to the other side. Their enemy didn't fare as well. In the middle of the army's pursuit on the sea's dry floor, Moses lowered his hands and the water walls collapsed, killing Pharaoh and his entire army.

Now, most of us haven't had an entire army with a neurotic leader chasing us with chariots. This is an extreme story showing the extreme powers of our God. But that should give us hope in what God is capable of when our enemy is pursuing us. Because let's face it, our enemy never stops his pursuit. Many times, it intensifies as we are biding our time in the wilderness, waiting on God to move on our behalf.

Take heart, my friend. God is in the victory business! He has no intention of bringing you to the wilderness only to let the enemy have victory. Even if the wilderness takes you to the bedside of a loved one or you are counting your change to buy a few groceries, you can depend on the fact that victory is coming. When you RSVP to yet another wedding as you think back on all your years as a single woman, be assured that victory is coming. The timing may be uncertain, but the triumph is not.

David, even after becoming king, experienced wilderness seasons and enemy attacks. After battling the Philistine and Gibeonite armies, he expressed his confidence in God by penning Psalm 18. Here's a promise we can hang our hat on until victory comes: "The LORD is my rock, my fortress and my deliverer; my God is my rock, in whom I take refuge, my shield and the horn of my salvation, my stronghold. I called to the LORD, who is worthy of praise, and I have been saved from my enemies" (vv. 2–3).

Survival Assurance #3: God Provides Everything I Need

When God *seems* silent and still, we begin to question His ability to handle our situation. Have no doubt—God is more than capable of taking care of us in our wilderness of waiting. God displayed His incomparable ability to provide for the Israelites before they ever walked out of the gates of Egypt. He made the Egyptians give them gold, jewels, and clothing. Today's street value of such plunder would be close to $42 million.

Can we agree this sent a strong assurance to the people? God showed His power with more than glittering gems and fine linens, though; He provided warmth, shade, and sustenance. As we read in Exodus, this is what the Israelites could count on as they waited in their wilderness:

> By day the LORD went ahead of them in a pillar of cloud to guide them on their way and by night in a pillar of fire to give them light, so that they could travel by day or night. (13:21)

> Then Moses stretched out his hand over the sea, and all that night the LORD drove the sea back with a strong east wind and turned it into dry land. The waters were divided. (14:21)

> Then the LORD said to Moses, "I will rain down bread from heaven for you. The people are to go out each day and gather enough for that day." (16:4)

> I will stand there before you by the rock at Horeb. Strike the rock, and water will come out of it for the people to drink. (17:6)

This is what we can count on in our wilderness wait:

> Because of the LORD's great love we are not
> consumed,
>   for his compassions never fail. (Lam. 3:22)

> And my God will meet all your needs according to
> the riches of his glory in Christ Jesus. (Phil. 4:19)

> And we know that in all things God works for the
> good of those who love him, who have been called
> according to his purpose. (Rom. 8:28)

> His divine power has given us everything we need
> for a godly life through our knowledge of him who
> called us by his own glory and goodness. (2 Pet. 1:3)

I could fill this entire book with scriptures that describe the ways we can count on God. Our great God is faithful and trustworthy to provide just what we need, right when we need it. In my head, I'm singing some old hymns, "Great Is Thy Faithfulness" and "Count Your Many Blessings." Won't you spend a minute or two praising God also? Sing out loud. You will be amazed at what it will do for your soul.

NO ABANDONMENT ISSUES HERE

We've talked at great length about the wilderness being a place where we *feel* as though God is no longer interested or active in our wait.

As far as we can tell, He's abandoned us. That's just not true. Take this to the bank and deposit it for safekeeping: God is always present with you. This characteristic of God is defined as being *omnipresent*. It's a big Bible word we can add to our vocabulary and retrieve when abandonment issues tiptoe into our thought life. Turn the corner of this page down and put a large star by this sentence: *Omnipresent* means always present; everywhere at the same time. Now, when you feel abandoned, remember to come back here and remind yourself that God is constantly, forever, eternally with you.

He is never *not* with me. He is never *not* with you. (English majors and grammar police, please don't email me about the double negatives.) He is next to us in our wilderness, even if we don't see Him at work. Whoa! I just blew my own mind.

Even though we *feel* abandoned by God, we aren't. God didn't abandon Abraham and Sarah. God didn't abandon the Israelites. God has not and will not abandon you. Try singing these words to the tune of "Jesus Loves Me, This I Know": "God is with me, this I know, for the Bible tells me so. Though His presence I can't see, God will not abandon me. Yes, God is with me. Yes, God is with me. Yes, God is with me. The Bible tells me so."

God didn't abandon David. He roamed in and out of caves and strongholds. He dodged arrows at the dinner table and fled from the king's army. For over fifteen years, he wandered and waited for his appointing. But David's wait did come to an end.

We know we're waiting well when we truly experience peace in God's pauses and plans. The peace is demonstrated in the resting of our thoughts and actions. Our real focus becomes a deep and abiding relationship with the Person of our faith, rather than manipulating our circumstances to receive the object of our wait. David waited well by focusing on God, not the problems, the people, or the palace.

THIS PRINCIPLE IN THEIR PAUSE

Ashley experienced momentum in speaking, writing, and teaching again after her early years of motherhood had passed. She wrote articles for her denominational newspaper, entered the blogosphere, signed a contract for a book on prayer, and spoke to local groups. She was reaching her goals. And then her father was diagnosed with terminal cancer. He encouraged her to keep going with her pursuits. Before long, he passed away. And everything stopped. She felt as though she had entered the wilderness for life. God felt silent. Instead of focusing on the Person of her faith to lead her out of the barren land, she fixed her thoughts back toward doubt. Doubt became her idol, which discouraged her from moving.

Samantha had witnessed others' waits throughout her life. Through their trials and tears, she gleaned wisdom on how to navigate the wilderness periods. This is one reason she served as a youth group leader, invested in others' marriages by babysitting and praying, and dove deep into studying Scripture. Each of these things nourished her sometimes-weary heart like bits of manna falling from the hand of God. To help herself avoid making her future husband or marriage an idol, Samantha planted her heart in the soil of this verse: "It is better to take refuge in the LORD than to trust in man" (Ps. 118:8 ESV). Finding comfort, confidence, and satisfaction in God increased her joy and took her focus off her desires. Serving and studying also helped prepare her to be a godly wife.

Dianna defines her wilderness experience as the dark night of the soul—but her soul was exposed to the holiness of God. When family members reacted to their circumstances with pride, doubt, fear, or discouragement, Dianna knew God was refining their hearts to be more like His Son's. Some idols were exposed, and she was challenged to turn to God only and to trust Him only.

Our story: Even though the mystery of Scott's health issue was solved and the old navy doctor at the clinic prescribed a medication that stabilized his eye infection, his depression led us to a wilderness. Learning to live with a chronic illness and being forced to make a career change were almost as difficult as the unknown health condition. After nearly a decade in the wilderness, the fog is lifting and the path ahead seems clearer. Even though rheumatoid arthritis looms over us, we both are doing what the Lord purposed us to do in our careers. Our relationships with the Lord are stronger, and there is once again joy in our marriage.

THIS PRINCIPLE IN YOUR PAUSE

Now it's your turn. Use the "Worth the Wait" pages in chapter 10 to examine your current wait in light of the lessons outlined in this chapter.

Here are some prompts to help you get started:

Discuss how the object of your wait has become an idol.

How can you apply the survival assurances to your wilderness experience?

Digging Deeper with David: Psalm 63

Read Psalm 63.

Many years after David took the throne, his son Absalom revolted against him (2 Sam. 15). Once again David was on the run from an enemy. How sad that this enemy was his own flesh and blood. He was forced from the comforts of the palace back to the isolation of the desert. He penned Psalm 63 in the dry desert lands surrounding his homeland of Judah. This landscape most certainly caused David to have physical thirst, and his desperation for water caused him to recognize his spiritual thirst and longing for the Lord. I wonder which would be worse—having spiritual thirst that could not be satisfied or having no spiritual thirst at all.

NOT THIRSTY AT ALL

For many years, each Sunday morning and most Wednesday nights you would find me in church. Thursday mornings or Sunday nights you would find me back at church leading a Bible study class. I was faithful, but I was not thirsty. Even though I was saved, I had never truly tasted the good ways of God.

Our salvation and our church involvement alone do not make us spiritually thirsty. If they did, our churches would be full to capacity. Budgets would have a surplus, and every people group in the world would have a missionary among them to share the gospel in their native tongue. It's simply impossible to thirst for something you have never really tasted.

David cried from the desert of Judah. I cried from the desert of my faith and marriage. Wanting things to be better, I attempted to quench my thirst my own way from one wrong place of refuge after another. Still thirsty and weary, I desperately cried out to God and asked for help.

Read Psalm 63:1.

Write the verse on the line below.

_____

The word *seek* is a challenging word. *Shachar* means "to seek early or diligently." And *diligently* means "the constant and attentive effort to accomplish anything." Our thirst will be filled by our attentive effort. But we must follow David's example and seek God, rather than our own ways, as a means to quench our thirst.

David spent time every morning seeking God's instructions and guidance (see, for example, Pss. 5:3; 59:16; and 65:1–8). I read of another man in the Bible who also spent time with God early every morning.

Read Mark 1:35.

What is the name of the man who prayed early in the morning?

_____

Those who have a thirst for God will be satisfied. And the more you thirst for God, the more you want God. You just have to have more! Will you make a commitment to seek God early in the morning?

SPIRITUAL THIRST~UNSATISFIED

David was experiencing worship withdrawal. He was forced not only to leave his home but also to lose access to the temple where he regularly worshipped God. He was unable to hear the temple choir sing or hear the instruments play. With his whole body and soul, he longed for God's house and worship.

Was it possible for David to worship God in the desert? Yes, and he did. We can worship God whenever and wherever we are, yet there is something powerful about worshipping in God's house with God's people.

A few years ago, my travel schedule kept me from my home church for several Sundays. When I returned home, I became ill and then shared the illness with my children. Before I knew it, I had missed six weeks of church. I was thirsty. Even though I had maintained my early quiet times, my thirst couldn't be satisfied until I was able to go to church and participate in corporate worship.

Read Psalm 84:10.

Where would David rather be than anywhere else?

_____

In this dry, barren land, David's mind thought of praising God. His praise gave his body life, his spirit hope, and his mind focus. In our life, we will know some desert experiences like David's. At times, we will be exiled from our normal life to the dry, barren land. But praise will revive our faith as nothing else will.

SPIRITUAL THIRST~SATISFIED

Are you thirsty for spiritual things? Do you long to say, "Better is one day in your courts" and "I have been in the sanctuary and beheld your power and glory"? In those times, when we cry out in our thirst, God offers us a drink that will never leave us thirsty.

Read John 4:13–14.

What is the result of drinking the water Jesus offers?

_____

This water of life is available through a personal relationship with Jesus Christ. Anyone who confesses "Lord, I believe" will be saved (see Rom. 10:9). When you recognize your need and ask for it to be filled, your thirst of salvation will be satisfied. This living water will not only satisfy your own thirst; it will also well up within you and spill out onto others. You will become a fountain of living water from which others can drink.

My friend, our God is just as ready to fill you up as He did David—and me. Just seek Him. Ask Him. He is more than willing to meet you in your dry and weary land.

9

When Our Waiting Ends . . . or Doesn't

I'm not sure where you are in your wait. Perhaps you've just begun to seek God to fulfill a brand-new dream. Maybe you have been wandering in the wilderness for decades. Perhaps you fall somewhere in between. How I wish we could end our journey of waiting together, each of us exclaiming, "I made it!" While some hear the crescendo begin and open their hands to receive the objects of their waits, others go on waiting.

Truth be told, our wait doesn't always end the way we dream it will. That can be tough to swallow. And that's why it is so important to develop and embrace a trusting relationship with God.

Things don't always turn out exactly as we planned,
but things always turn out as God planned.

Our wait has equipped us to develop and embrace a trusting relationship with God. This relationship is our solid foundation that enables us to withstand the ebb and flow of each wait. It serves as a soothing balm for the sting of disappointment when our wait doesn't end as we've hoped and will sustain us if more waiting is required.

Things don't always turn out exactly as *we* planned, but things always turn out as *God* planned. The Bible is full of real people with real waits and unexpected endings. Moses faithfully led the Israelites from the agony of slavery to the joy of freedom at the edge of the Promised Land, but he wasn't permitted to enter (Num. 20:12). Jacob fell in love with Rachel. He served her father, Laban, for seven years as a means to earn her hand in marriage. On his long-awaited wedding day, he received quite a shock. His bride removed her veil in the wedding tent, and instead of seeing Rachel's beautiful face, he stood looking at her sister, Leah. Laban had tricked Jacob, and the young man would have to work another seven years for his father-in-law before he would finally be able to marry Rachel (Gen. 29).

What about Noah? He worked through a 120-year wait before the flood came, exactly as God said it would. Israel's king, David, waited more than fifteen years. And Jesus? He waited thirty years to start His earthly ministry. He served as He waited for God's perfect plan of redemption to come to fruition. He was crucified, placed in a tomb, rose from the dead, and ascended to heaven, just as God planned.

To encourage you through your wait and its ending, a few of my friends will now share their stories of their waits.

SOMETIMES THE WAIT ENDS IN SORROW

Becky and her husband, C. T., have committed their lives to full-time ministry. C. T. preaches the Word of God with intense love and excitement, and he and Becky share their gifted voices in worship with people all over the country. They prayed to be blessed with a child—and they were. Tucker was the first Townsend baby. A little over a year after Tucker arrived, C. T. and Becky received the exciting news that she was pregnant with another son, Cashton Isaac.

Becky's second pregnancy was seamless—until it suddenly wasn't. During a routine checkup, Becky's joy turned to weeping as she learned unborn Cashton had hydrops fetalis and his death in utero was imminent.

The following weeks, Becky and C. T. went from one specialist to another, desperate to hear a better prognosis. They called on their church family and friends to fast and pray for God to spare Cashton's life. The couple refused to heed the counsel of some physicians who advised them to terminate the pregnancy and instead chose to believe in the Great Physician, Jehovah Rapha, God the Healer. C. T. and Becky put their complete trust in the God who had formed little Cashton in Becky's womb, perfectly knitting him together.

Several months later, the young parents' wait came to an end. Becky gave birth to Cashton's small, still body; his soul had gone to be with the Lord months before. C. T. and Becky's wait ended in sorrow and heartache. They grieve as parents who have hope that their son is living eternally with his heavenly Father. God carried them through the valley of the shadow of death. Now, they are able to share the hope of Jesus in a way they didn't know before Cashton.

C. T. and Becky remained in their pasture of ministry and pressed through their pain to continue to serve the Lord. Tucker is now a big brother to Syler, and the boys recently welcomed home their baby sister, Everlee Carolyn. Things don't always turn out exactly as *we* planned, but things always turn out as *God* planned.

SOMETIMES THE WAIT ENDS BETTER THAN EXPECTED

In 2005, Glynnis and her husband, Tod, adopted two little girls from Liberia. The girls were eight and ten but were the size of five-year-olds. They had never been in school and had never seen running water. The deprivation they had experienced was significant. But Glynnis, Tod, and their three sons were convinced that with enough love and time, the missing pieces would be filled in.

It quickly became apparent that other issues were brewing. The challenges facing the family were immense, as they learned the older daughter had a cognitive disability and severe hearing loss in one ear. The younger girl's issues ran even deeper with past abuse and neglect, causing significant emotional damage and life-altering behavioral issues.

Expecting some challenges, Glynnis had cut back on her work, teaching, and public speaking for a period of three years. But three years wasn't going to be enough. So Glynnis said good-bye to travel, a public teaching ministry, and book writing, certain she would have to travel and speak for a publisher to believe in her.

Life was hard in the Whitwer home, as they faced one diagnosis after another and traveled from therapist to therapist and doctor to doctor. The emotional trauma of the younger daughter affected all of them, and Glynnis maintained her focus on her family for years.

Although Glynnis longed to serve God through her work at Proverbs 31 Ministries and through her book writing and public speaking, it seemed He had other plans.

God could see something coming that Glynnis never saw. He saw the world of the Internet opening up opportunities for women to minister from home. No longer did authors have to travel and speak to get a book contract. Emerging were new ways to write, teach, and minister to women that hadn't been available before.

As Glynnis submitted her dreams to God, He repackaged them and gave them back to her. God opened up opportunities for her to move to an executive position within Proverbs 31 Ministries even though she lives two thousand miles from the home office. God established COMPEL Training, where Glynnis gets to teach monthly to over fifteen hundred authors, and He has blessed her with multiple book contracts so she can fulfill her dream to write.

In one of the sweetest acts, God gave her the title executive director of communications. Now, that might not seem so special on the surface, but when Glynnis was studying public relations in college, her dream job was director of communications for a company. Although Glynnis never told anyone about this dream, God obviously never forgot. She is convinced the addition of "executive" in her title was a wink from Him ... almost as if God was saying, "See, Glynnis, I got you."

SOMETIMES THE WAIT ENDS DIFFERENT THAN EXPECTED

Chad and Heather were schoolmates, but they didn't realize they were soul mates until they reconnected after college. The two fell in love, married, and started their life together. After two years of learning the balance and rhythm of the dance called marriage, they decided to start a family. What seemed to be easy for everyone else proved difficult for Heather and Chad.

They tried to conceive for over a year without success. Heather went to a specialist to determine the cause of her infertility. The doctor didn't hesitate to start her on medication to ensure conception. Within three months, Heather became pregnant. The doctors monitored her closely as her low hormone production could cause complications to her pregnancy.

At her eight-week checkup, an ultrasound revealed an ectopic pregnancy. Heartbroken, Heather sought refuge in her church. She took her grief to the altar. Heather soaked the carpet with her tears and filled the air with questions, begging God for help. And it wasn't long before peace swept over her like a wave. Heather had lost her baby, but not her hope.

With the doctor's consent and a three-month wait, Heather and Chad began the process again. Another miracle! She conceived without any fertility medications. They couldn't have been more thrilled. Like before, her body failed to produce sufficient hormones, but supplements seemed to help. But a few months into her pregnancy, she found herself in the ER fighting for her life. Lying in a hospital bed on Christmas Eve, she lost one of the most precious gifts she'd been given, her baby.

Again Heather conceived, and again she miscarried. I know at this point your heart aches for the Wilsons. But their story doesn't end in the wilderness of miscarriages. Sometimes things work out differently from the way *we* plan, but they always work out exactly as *God* plans.

Through circumstances only God could design, the Wilsons are now a family of four. Heather and Chad welcomed Trevor into their lives through the gift of adoption. A woman they didn't know chose life for her baby, and she sacrificially entrusted her little boy to Chad and Heather. It was as if God split the heavens, reached down, and hand delivered this precious gift. Three years later, another selfless momma delivered a baby girl—Sydney—whom the Wilsons are delighted to call their daughter.

The Wilsons will tell you nothing about their five-year wait felt easy. But they have unmistakably seen the mighty movement of a mighty God. In Heather's words, "Our children are every bit as much ours as they would have been if they had come from our own flesh. God has reconfirmed time and time again that they are a gift."

The wait might be hard. The wait might be long. The wait might not end by receiving the long-awaited object. But what God does give is always worth the wait even if it is not what we longed for. Let's take a look at the culmination of David's wait and what the Lord had in store for him.

DAVID'S WAIT ENDS

It seems like just yesterday that we stood at the pasture's edge watching Samuel pour anointing oil over young David's head. It's hard to believe we have traveled almost fifteen years of David's life. We hid with him in caves, sat with him at the dinner table when he almost lost his life, and we were privy to his intimate conversations. We have cheered him on, and now we witness his wait end as we hear the pomp and circumstance of his inauguration ceremony.

In 2 Samuel we read, "After this, David asked the LORD, 'Should I move back to one of the towns of Judah?'" (2:1 NLT). After what? A war-torn and heartbroken David sought the Lord's wisdom after fighting the Amalekites and losing Jonathan, his best friend and confidant, and Saul, his king. The crescendo of David's wait rose as the body of his best friend fell. While David battled the Amalekites, King Saul and Jonathan warred with the Philistines. Jonathan was overtaken and killed by a Philistine. King Saul knew his army would not win and his time had come. Not wanting to die at the hands of the enemy, King Saul fell on his own sword, taking his life. In an instant, Israel had no king, and David's wait had come to a close.

After this, the Lord instructed David to move his family to Hebron. While the troops anointed him king of Judah, the people of Israel proclaimed Saul's son Ishbosheth king of Israel. Warring between Judah and Israel went on for years until David was finally crowned king over *all* of Israel.

Waiting for a life he never dreamed of or asked for was finally a reality after nearly twenty years. At last, all was well in David's world.

POST-WAIT RELATIONSHIP PROTECTORS

We've gained a wealth of knowledge from David about waiting well. He most assuredly lived out the main principle of *Wait and See*: he never exchanged the Person of his faith with the object of his wait. Waiting well isn't all we can learn from David, though.

We should take certain steps to protect our relationship with the Lord after our wait ends. We should also follow these steps if our waiting doesn't end. Let's look to see how David handled life after a few years of sitting on the throne. We'll learn that even after our wait is over, it's vital to continue to keep our focus on the Person of our faith. As we'll find out from David, a once-nurtured relationship with God can easily slip into a neglected one.

Post-Wait, Still-Waiting Relationship Protector #1: Stay in the Word and Stay on Our Knees

Scripture never specifically points to a decline in David's relationship with God, but his actions speak louder than words. Our post-wait relationship with God has to be protected. Our parched days in the wilderness and lonely nights in the pastures need to remain fresh in our mind. It is in these places we learned how to be close to God, to defeat our enemy, and to celebrate who He created us to be.

Spending time with God every day is the only way to preserve our precious relationship with Him that we cultivated during our wait. What are some ways we can do this? His Word is our compass. Reading it every day will keep us in alignment with His plan. Prayer is our connection to God. We pray in the power of the Holy Spirit to God the Father. Without these essentials, nurture becomes neglect.

We're most vulnerable when we're least nourished.

Although David never exchanged God for the object of his wait, somewhere along the way his communication with God broke down. The decline started when David showed disregard for God's definition of marriage by having more than one wife. This exposed David's weakness and vulnerability to sins of the flesh. We're most vulnerable when we're least nourished. Perhaps Paul said it best in Galatians 5:16: "So I say, let the Holy Spirit guide your lives. Then you won't be doing what your sinful nature craves" (NLT). Staying close to God by staying deep in His Word starves our sinful cravings and nourishes our spirit.

Post-Wait, Still-Waiting Relationship Protector #2: Be Where We Should Be, Doing What We Should Be Doing

Sin is as slippery as an eel. A healthy, nourished spirit enables us to recognize sin when it crouches at our door. David's spirit was already weak when sin crouched at his door (or rather, on the roof). "Late one afternoon, after his midday rest, David got out of bed and was walking on the roof of the palace. As he looked out over the city, he noticed a woman of unusual beauty taking a bath" (2 Sam. 11:2 NLT).

David saw a beautiful woman bathing. Overwhelmed by her beauty, he sent an official to attain her identity. Even after discovering she was Bathsheba, wife of Uriah, a soldier in his army, and daughter of Eliam, one of his mighty men, David had her brought to the palace and slept with her. Oh, how I wish the story ended there!

One sin usually begets more sins; such is the case of David's sin with Bathsheba. After learning Bathsheba had become pregnant, David commanded Uriah to be sent to the front lines of battle to ensure his death. David, the anointed one, was now an adulterous murderer.

David's sin with Bathsheba was a sin of opportunity. David stumbled upon, and seized, this opportunity because he was not where he was supposed to be: "In the spring, at the time when kings go off to war, David sent Joab out with the king's men and the whole Israelite army. They destroyed the Ammonites and besieged Rabbah. But David remained in Jerusalem" (2 Sam. 11:1).

That last sentence speaks volumes. David stayed in Jerusalem, but he should have gone to war with his men. So much wrong can happen when we are not where we are supposed to be. David compromised his integrity and brought shame on his name. His actions redirected the future of his lineage forever.

Post-Wait, Still-Waiting Relationship Protector #3: Be Real with Ourselves and God Concerning Sin

Nearly a year had passed since David took Bathsheba as his own wife. Their first child was about to be born, but David had yet to ask God for forgiveness. His lack of remorse displeased the Lord, so God sent Nathan to call on the king to urge him to confess and repent.

As you can imagine, the scene wasn't pretty. Nathan not only confronted David with his sin, but the prophet also announced God's punishment. David's iniquity changed the course of his family forever. God took David's immorality as a personal affront, and He pronounced that the family line would see continued violence and bloodshed. "From this time on, your family will live by the sword because you have despised me by taking Uriah's wife to be your own" (2 Sam. 12:10 NLT). What a sobering moment this must have been for David. Overwrought by guilt and shame, he exclaimed, "I have sinned against the LORD" (2 Sam. 12:13 NLT).

We can fall so deeply into the abyss of sin that we are unable to see truth. Our propensity is not to take sinfulness seriously, especially if we don't see its direct harm or consequences. Such an approach numbs us to sin's reality. When we're in this place, we desperately need God's help to open our eyes and lead us to repentance. Otherwise, we create a chasm in our relationship with the Lord.

David didn't remain in his sin; he confessed it. God forgave and remained faithful to him as he governed the nation of Israel. He didn't waver in His promises. David's faithful God is our faithful God. He forgives our sin just as He forgave David's. How reassuring to read, "If we confess our sins, he is faithful and just and will forgive us our sins and purify us from all unrighteousness" (1 John 1:9).

THE PROTECTION OF MY PAUSE

Five years, ten months, and fourteen days constitute the length of one of my pauses—the one I told you about in chapter 8 when I crafted an idol in the form of a book. It's only fitting that we end our journey together by finishing that story. Not one of my finer moments, I must say. As I charged full-steam ahead, God pressed pause.

On this side of the pause, I can clearly see God's protection; however, that is not how I saw it then. I would love to tell you that I acted humbly and joyfully frolicked around the pasture as I waited. That would be a lie. I accepted my friend's counsel—sort of. *I* wanted to publish a book so *I* continued to try. Every time an agent or publisher turned down my book proposal, the wound of rejection deepened. For years, I carried a two-ton chip on my shoulder that I did my best to disguise.

The pause created real trust issues for me with God. *Why did You call me into ministry only to allow me to fail? I thought You created me for more than this.* Eventually I stopped writing and I quit trying to get a book published. It was time to take down my idol and ask God's forgiveness for focusing on the object of my wait instead of Him. As I packed away my book ideas, Satan whispered the same old lies: *I told you that you aren't good enough. You were foolish to have even tried.*

Though my writing ministry had come to a standstill, my speaking ministry continued. At a retreat in Granbury, Texas, each woman was given a three-by-five index card with the words *And by Faith* across the top. They were to write something for which they would trust God. As the speaker, I did not expect to participate with the guests and complete a card. But what I expect and what God plans are not always the same.

Holding the card in the air, I gave the audience instructions. I tucked the card into my Bible and went to my seat as a song played. The still, small voice of the Holy Spirit whispered, "Trust Me with your ministry, the book, and speaking." The Lord bid me to complete a card.

As the worship team continued to sing, I continued to offer excuses as to why I couldn't write those words on a card. I even pulled the old "I don't have a pen" excuse. I wasn't entirely sure I wanted to put it all in His hands. Like *everything* wasn't already there. (Humor me here.)

With fear and trembling, I borrowed a pen from the woman beside me, and I wrote the words, "Trust Me with your ministry, the book, and speaking." I tucked the card into my Bible. There. (Insert deep sigh.) I had done it. After I returned home from Texas, the pause continued ... for years.

Occasionally, over the years, I would run across the card when I emptied my Bible of church bulletins and gum wrappers. With doubt in my heart, I'd read the card and want to toss it out with the trash but couldn't let myself. I'm not sure why. I just couldn't throw the card away.

Before the Granbury retreat, I thought I was done with writing. But over the years, my heart began to soften toward writing again. I took a step out of my comfort zone and attended a writing conference with some friends. I was nervous and felt out of place, as published authors surrounded me—my friends, the speakers, other attendees. Everyone seemed to have manuscripts, publishers, and bestsellers. And though one speaker after another made their way to the stage to encourage us in our writing, I was feeling anything but encouraged ... until a Christian fiction author spoke.

Because fiction is not my genre, I only half-listened to his message as I doodled. Then he said something that captured my attention: "Before enlightenment, chop wood and draw water. After enlightenment, chop wood and draw water."[16] *What does chopping wood and drawing water have to do with writing?* I listened more intently. "If you want to be a good writer, write," he said. "Before you get published, write. After you get published, write." These words brought life to my pause.

Determined to practice and improve my craft, I went home to "chop wood and draw water." I stayed within my pastures, tended to my sheep, and continued to work out my salvation. My writing would *not* become an idol again.

Over the next several years, I submitted multiple book proposals. The "thanks, but no thanks" letters came one after another. Once again, I faced defeat and rejection. This time *Depression, Discouragement,* and *Doubt* whispered but did not have victory. My eyes were on God, not myself or my publishing ambitions. I trusted the timing and outcome to Him, which deflected the rejection. I sensed God telling me to write, and write I did. Then one day, a different sort of letter came from a publishing house.

You're smart. You know what I'm going to say. You hold in your hands the end of my wait. (Insert my tears.)

Five years. Ten months. Fourteen days.

On March 9, 2015, I opened my mailbox to find a legal-sized envelope containing the return on my investment, a contract for two books. I'd waited 2,144 days after I reluctantly tucked the scribbled card in my Bible for my pause to come to an end. There's so much more to tell, but the details aren't that important.

We're friends now, right? Can I ask you something? Has God asked you to trust Him—to give Him the object of your wait? Is it a dream tucked in your heart that only you and He know about? Are you waiting for your prodigal to return? For your husband or child to be saved? For a job? For a disease-free body? Will you give Him your wait today?

You may be thinking, *It's easy for you to say all that. Your card was answered. Your wait is over. But would you be saying all this trustworthy and faithful stuff if the envelope hadn't come in the mail?*

Yes. Yes, I would. God is never *not* trustworthy. He is never *not* faithful. (I know, again with the double negatives.) Even when the envelope doesn't show up, He does.

He is trustworthy! He is faithful! You are holding the proof.

Now, stay in your pasture, work out your salvation, move when He says move, and never exchange the object of your wait for the Person of your faith.

Wait well, my friend. Wait well.

THIS PRINCIPLE IN THEIR PAUSE

Ashley trusted God through a long season of grief. She gave permission to let herself be still in her weakness and let God bind her broken heart. She didn't rush the process. She kept her eyes on the God of her salvation, the God of her calling. At present, she is moving forward. She founded a mom's Bible study group in her church. She is speaking to women's groups again, and God is enlarging her ministry. Through losing her father, she can now minister to women of all ages about grief. Her pause experiences have strengthened her faith and given her the ability to identify with women around her who are in seasons of waiting. God never wasted time during the waiting but taught her lessons about patience, humility, and how to depend on Him. She has learned that waiting is the root of the Christian life.

Samantha rejoiced as her wait ended seven months after she met her husband through an online dating site. Some of the first attributes he fell in love with were her knowledge of the Bible and her heart to serve others—two things she specifically nurtured during her wait. At the beginning of their dating relationship, Samantha discovered that one of Josh's favorite Bible verses is also Micah 6:8. He now has it tattooed in place of a wedding ring as a reminder for them every day. They read Scripture, pray, and serve together as they sharpen each other. While being married is *a* delight of her life, her relationship with Jesus—which grew as she waited—remains *the* joy of her life. Neither Samantha nor her husband would have it any other way.

Dianna endured a six-year wait. The toll it took on her family was heartbreaking, but the gain with God was well worth it. God made sure of it. Her husband is working in his dream job with the people in the city that he loves. Her son is now in college studying music and worship. Her daughter is in nursing school with compassion and mercy rooted in her heart. Dianna continues to faithfully serve and love her family and her God, praising Him for deliverance and for her time in the wait.

Our story: I am confident my desire for Scott's healing is within God's will; however, I do not know if He will deliver Scott from this illness before or after he meets the Lord face to face. Either way, we know it is not predicated on either his or my ability to pray, the length of time we read our Bibles each day, or how hard we work. We just have to keep doing what we know to do and trust that my husband's healing—should it come this side of heaven or not—is based on the grace of God. We've shifted our focus to the truth that even on the bad days, God is still good, and He will carry us through this season of waiting just as He carried us through the last one.

THIS PRINCIPLE IN YOUR PAUSE

Now it's your turn. Use the "Worth the Wait" pages in chapter 10 to examine your current wait in light of the lessons outlined in this chapter.

Here are some prompts to help you get started:

Write your own *And by Faith* statement. Record the date and time.

How will you protect your post-wait, still-waiting relationship with God?

Digging Deeper with David: Psalm 19

Read Psalm 19.

As we have studied David's songs and read his story, there is one last takeaway we can tuck into our heart. Whether our wait ends or we are still waiting, God is good. This statement is as difficult to write as it is to read. While you hold in your hands the object of one of my waits, my heart continues to trust the Person of my faith for the outcome of other waits.

In Psalm 19, David's eloquent words challenge us to see God's majesty in creation, in Scripture, and through a right standing with Him. Continuing to look toward God and believe in His goodness is the only way to preserve our now-secure relationship with the Lord.

LOOK UPWARD TO HIS CREATION AND EXPERIENCE HIM (VV. 1–6)

A few years ago, my morning quiet times with the Lord became routine and needed new life. *What is wrong? What has changed?* My heart was heavy and longed to be closer to Him. In true David style, I took my concerns to the Lord. I kept meeting with the Lord and waiting for resolution to my concerns. Not long after, I felt an overwhelming desire to be outside. This might not seem like an aha moment to those of you outdoorsy types, but to this indoor girl, I knew God had given me the answer to my prayer. I needed to *get out*.

My morning quiet times and I moved outside. The fresh connection to God was immediate. With my Bible resting on my lap and praise music bellowing in my ears, I celebrated His greatness while sitting in His creation. Talk about wow moments with God!

God's creation plays a symphony of praise that sounds all day. His works of art are on display for our pleasure. He clearly communicates His message and His majesty through creation.

Read Romans 1:20.

What has God made clearly known through creation?

_____

LOOK TOWARD HIS WORD TO HEAR FROM HIM (VV. 7-11)

The Law. Statutes. Precepts. Commands. These lofty Bible words sound weighty and burdensome even to the most brilliant Bible scholar. It's easy to conjure pictures of Old Testament sacrifices and prophets standing in tunics reading from scrolls. Don't feel bad if you have these thoughts about God's Word. Less than a decade ago I felt the exact same way.

Guilt and shame consumed me because, while I love God, I didn't love His Word. I couldn't imagine how a C student could ever understand the Scriptures, much less live them. Then I learned two verses that radically changed my pessimistic thinking.

Read 2 Timothy 3:16–17.

Why do we have Scripture anyway?

_____

_____

God left His Word to teach us how to live and to complete the work He assigns to us. The assignment may be serving in the church nursery, working on the mission field, or staying home to care for your kids and husband. God has a good work for everyone. Learning and living His Word equips us for His work.

Deuteronomy 29:29 radically changed my view of God's Word: "The LORD our God has secrets known to no one. We are not accountable for them, but we and our children are accountable forever for all that he has revealed to us, so that we may obey all the terms of these instructions" (NLT). Friend, we are not accountable for what God does not reveal. God will reveal what He wants us to know. This C student lives in this freedom every day!

God's ways give life and the security we need to live out His plan before, during, and after the wait.

Using Psalm 119, complete the following to discover some of the benefits of keeping God's Word.

When we walk according to His Word, we …

Verse 1 _____

Verse 11 _____

Verse 45 _____

Verse 54 _____

Verse 165 _____

LOOK INWARD TO BECOME MORE LIKE HIM

Looking inward isn't pleasant. It's much easier to blame our unpleasant circumstances on others. We learned in chapter 3 that God gets personal so we can know Him personally. By looking inward, we allow the Holy Spirit to expose the parts of our lives that aren't pleasing to God. This affords us the opportunity to repent and reshape these areas to be more Christlike.

Read Genesis 1:27.

In whose image were you created?

_____

From a former inside girl, step outside today. Have no agenda other than to listen to His creation praise His name. You can even join in the song. Then maybe tomorrow you can repeat the process with your Bible in your lap. Breathe deeply and ask the Lord to help cooperate with the work of His Word and the Holy Spirit so you can become more like Him.

10

Worth the Wait: My Story

INTRODUCTION

What is my current wait? Include specifics. How long have I been waiting? What are my feelings about my wait and its length?

_____

_____

_____

_____

_____

_____

_____

_____

_____

_____

_____

_____

CHAPTER 1

In what ways am I rushing through my wait? What *misconception* resonates most with me? Do I really believe that God is good and His blessings are not dependent on my "works"?

Misconception #1: I must not have heard God correctly.

Misconception #2: I must desire something not in God's will for my life.

Misconception #3: I must not be praying enough.

Misconception #4: I must not have enough faith.

Misconception #5: I must not be working hard enough.

_____

_____

_____

_____

_____

_____

_____

_____

_____

_____

_____

_____

_____

_____

_____

CHAPTER 2

What steps am I currently taking to love God more? What ways do I show love to others? Are there ways I can do more for others while staying true to the pasture God has assigned me to?

_____

_____

_____

_____

_____

_____

_____

_____

_____

_____

_____

_____

_____

_____

_____

_____

_____

_____

_____

_____

_____

_____

CHAPTER 3

Start by praying the following verses from Psalm 139 (THE MESSAGE):

"GOD, investigate my life; get all the facts firsthand. I'm an open book to you; even from a distance, you know what I'm thinking" (vv. 1–2).

"Investigate my life, O God, find out everything about me; cross-examine and test me, get a clear picture of what I'm about; See for yourself whether I've done anything wrong—then guide me on the road to eternal life" (vv. 23–24).

How can I make my heart soft toward God's work in my life? In what ways is He changing my heart? How is He teaching me humility?

_____

_____

_____

_____

_____

_____

_____

_____

_____

_____

_____

_____

_____

_____

CHAPTER 4

How do I respond when God asks me to move and/or change? What is God asking me to change? What is the greatest obstacle I face? Wavering? Fear? Confidence? Selfishness? Unbelief? Am I obeying or delaying?

_____

_____

_____

_____

_____

_____

_____

_____

_____

_____

_____

_____

_____

_____

_____

_____

_____

_____

_____

_____

CHAPTER 5

What are my right places of refuge? What are my wrong places of refuge, and how can I walk away from them? How do I fight the enemies that seek to distract me as I wait?

_____

_____

_____

_____

_____

_____

_____

_____

_____

_____

_____

_____

_____

_____

_____

_____

_____

_____

_____

_____

CHAPTER 6

Who has God brought into my life to help me as I wait? How have they helped? If I feel abandoned, like nobody cares, I can write a prayer asking God to help me recognize and accept the help He wants to give.

_____

_____

_____

_____

_____

_____

_____

_____

_____

_____

_____

_____

_____

_____

_____

_____

_____

_____

_____

_____

_____

CHAPTER 7

When I consider how the *Uninviteds* have intruded in my story, how willing, armed, and right minded do I believe I am? What can I do to strengthen my warfare?

_____

_____

_____

_____

_____

_____

_____

_____

_____

_____

_____

_____

_____

_____

_____

_____

_____

_____

_____

_____

_____

CHAPTER 8

How can I apply the survival strategies to my wilderness experience?
How has the object of my wait become an idol?

_____

_____

_____

_____

_____

_____

_____

_____

_____

_____

_____

_____

_____

_____

_____

_____

_____

_____

_____

_____

_____

CHAPTER 9

Below I will write my own *And by Faith* statement, complete with the date and time. How will I protect my post-wait, still-waiting relationship with God?

_____

_____

_____

_____

_____

_____

_____

_____

_____

_____

_____

_____

_____

_____

_____

_____

_____

_____

_____

_____

_____

Epilogue

The Story of the Butterfly

A man found a cocoon of a butterfly. One day a small opening appeared. He sat and watched the butterfly for several hours as it struggled to force its body through that little hole. Then it seemed to stop making any progress. It appeared as if it had gotten as far as it could, and it could go no further.

So the man decided to help the butterfly. He took a pair of scissors and snipped off the remaining bit of the cocoon.

The butterfly then emerged easily. But it had a swollen body and small, shriveled wings.

The man continued to watch the butterfly because he expected that, at any moment, the wings would enlarge and expand to be able to support the body, which would contract in time.

Neither happened! In fact, the butterfly spent the rest of its life crawling around with a swollen body and shriveled wings. It never was able to fly.

What the man, in his kindness and haste, did not understand was that the restricting cocoon and the struggle required for the butterfly to get through the tiny opening were Life's way of forcing fluid from the body of the butterfly into its wings so that it would be ready for flight once it achieved its freedom from the cocoon.

Sometimes struggles are exactly what we need in our lives. Remember nature needs no help, just no interference. There are processes of life, things we all go through. The struggles are a part of our journey and are preparing us for what awaits. They are preparing us to fly.

—Author unknown

I have loved every single minute of my time with you! As you turn the last pages, I'd like to leave you with one final word, well, four final words: *don't rush the wait*. Please, dear friend, don't rush your wait. Let the pressure of the wait strengthen your faith as the tightness of the cocoon strengthened the butterfly's wings.

Through the struggle of breaking free, its wings were made strong so when it was released the world could see its beautiful colors.

Let your wait fortify your faith, cultivate your character, and reinforce your resolve so that when you fly away from it, the world will see the beautiful colors of your faith.

In His Great Love,
Wendy

Appendix

Working Out While You Wait

In chapter 2, we unpacked this awesome verse in Philippians:

> Therefore, my dear friends, as you have always obeyed—not only in my presence, but now much more in my absence—continue to work out your salvation with fear and trembling. (2:12)

Remember we work *out* our salvation, not work *for* our salvation. The work we do for the kingdom of God is a result of the work Christ has done in our life through the work of the Holy Spirit. The more we love God, the more we will love others. Our actions will be an outpouring of the wellspring of love in our hearts.

Maybe like me, your heart is full and you want to serve, to work out your salvation while you wait but don't know where to start. I have provided an "in the meantime" list with suggestions of places to serve with local and national organizations.

LOCAL SERVICES

- Pregnancy centers
- Adoption agencies
- Homeless shelters
- Nursing homes
- Schools
- Mentoring programs
- Women's shelters
- Foster care
- Hospitals
- Your church
- Election board
- Food pantries

NATIONAL SERVICES

- National Right to Life: www.nrlc.org
- American Red Cross: www.redcross.org
- Compassion International: www.compassion.com
- Meals on Wheels: www.mealsonwheelsamerica.org
- Samaritan's Purse: www.samaritanspurse.org
- National Hospice and Palliative Care: www.nhpco.org

Notes

1. "G. Campbell Morgan Quotes," Goodreads.com, accessed May 19, 2016, www.goodreads.com/author/quotes/366790.G_Campbell_Morgan.

2. "Entry for Strong's #5156," StudyLight.org, accessed May 20, 2016, www.studylight.org /lexicons/greek/gwview.cgi?n=5156.

3. "Strong's Number 5156," StudyLight.org, accessed May 20, 2016, http://classic .studylight.org/lex/grk/view.cgi?number=5156.

4. David Guzik, "Philippians 2: Humble Living in Light of Jesus's Humbling Example," *Guzik Bible Commentary*, Bible Hub, accessed May 20, 2016, http://biblehub.com/commentaries/guzik/commentaries/5002.htm.

5. Chrystal Evans Hurst, "The Stranger on the Bench," Proverbs 31 Ministries, October 8, 2014, http://proverbs31.org/devotions/devo/the-stranger-on-the-bench.

6. C. S. Lewis, *Mere Christianity* (United Kingdom: Geoffrey Bles, 1952).

7. David Guzik, "1 Corinthians 1: Jesus, the Wisdom of God," *Guzik Bible Commentary*, Bible Hub, accessed May 20, 2016, http://biblehub.com/commentaries/guzik /1_corinthians/1.htm.

8. "Bible Timeline: Exodus," Bible Hub, accessed May 20, 2016, http://biblehub.com/ timeline/exodus/1.htm.

9. "Strong's Concordance: 5287," Bible Hub, accessed May 20, 2016, http://biblehub.com /greek/5287.htm.

10. Beth Moore, *Believing God: Experiencing a Fresh Explosion of Faith*, video (Nashville: LifeWay, 2003).

11. "Matthew Henry's Commentary: 1 Samuel 27," Bible Hub, accessed May 20, 2016, http://biblehub.com/commentaries/mhc/1_samuel/27.htm.

12. David Guzik, "1 Samuel 18: Conflict between Saul and David," *Guzik Bible Commentary*, Bible Hub, accessed May 20, 2016, http://biblehub.com /commentaries/guzik/1_samuel/18.htm.

13. David Guzik, "Isaiah 54: The Restoration of Israel, the Wife of the LORD," *Guzik Bible Commentary*, Bible Hub, accessed May 20, 2016, http://biblehub .com/commentaries/guzik/isaiah/54.htm.

14. Dictionary.com, s.v. "idolatry," accessed May 20, 2016, http://dictionary.reference .com/browse/idolatry?s=t.

15. "How Did the Israelites Cast a Golden Calf by Mount Sinai," Bible Answer Stand, accessed May 20, 2016, http://bibleanswerstand.org/QA_calf.htm.

16. Ted Dekker, Re:Write Conference, Austin, TX, October, 13, 2013.

About the Author

Wendy is the wife of Scott, mother of Blaire and Griffin, author, speaker, and Bible study teacher. She loves lazy Sundays watching golf with her husband, thrift-store shopping with her daughter, and watching building shows with her son.

Wendy is the author of *Wait and See*. She is a contributing author to the *Real-Life Women's Devotional Bible, Encouragement for Today: Devotions for Daily Living, The Reason We Speak*, and *God's Purpose for Every Woman*. Wendy writes devotions for Proverbs 31 Ministries' *Encouragement for Today* and is a content provider for the free online devotion app First 5 as well as a member of the Proverbs 31 Ministries speaker team.

She leads women all over the world to life change through her in-depth online Bible studies. She has led thousands of women through her *Read through the Word* study of the One Chronological Bible. Down-to-earth and transparent, Wendy teaches in such a way that women feel she is speaking directly to their hearts.

Her messages are filled with biblical insights but sprinkled with just the right amount of humor to help her audiences see she is a real, everyday woman. Wendy inspires her audiences to:

- make spending time in God's Word each day a priority;
- look for God working around them every day; and
- view life with a God-first perspective.

To bring the message of *Wait and See* or another of Wendy's inspiring topics to your next event, contact speakercoordinator@proverbs31.org.

Connect with Wendy:

Website: wendypope.org
Email: wendy@wendypope.org
Facebook: www.facebook.com/wendypope67
Twitter: @wendybpope
Instagram: Wendy_Pope
Pinterest: www.pinterest.com/wendypope67
YouTube   www.youtube.com/user/wendypope

ABOUT PROVERBS 31 MINISTRIES

If you were inspired by *Wait and See* and desire to deepen your own personal relationship with Jesus Christ, I encourage you to connect with Proverbs 31 Ministries.

We exist to be a trusted friend who will take you by the hand and walk by your side, leading you one step closer to the heart of God through:

- Free online daily devotions
- Online Bible studies
- Daily radio program
- Books and resources
- Free First 5 app

For more information about Proverbs 31 Ministries, visit: www .Proverbs31.org.

Bible Credits